# HE OPENED THE DOOR OF JAPAN

BOOKS BY

## CARL CROW

•

400 MILLION CUSTOMERS

I SPEAK FOR THE CHINESE

MASTER KUNG

HE OPENED THE DOOR OF JAPAN

•

*Harper & Brothers*
*Publishers*

Townsend Harris

# HE OPENED THE DOOR OF JAPAN

*Townsend Harris and the Story of
His Amazing Adventures in Establishing
American Relations with the Far East*

BY

## CARL CROW

ILLUSTRATED

HARPER & BROTHERS PUBLISHERS

NEW YORK AND LONDON

1939

TO

## DR. MARIO EMILIO COSENZA

*in appreciation of his untiring and unselfish efforts
to preserve the memory of Townsend Harris.*

# CONTENTS

# ILLUSTRATIONS

ix

# PREFACE

IT HAS been a pleasant and an inspiring task to write the
life of Townsend Harris; pleasant to think that I
should have an opportunity to introduce him to his fellow-
Americans; inspiring to record the success of a man who
triumphed over so many difficulties. It might also have
been a dispiriting and discouraging task had I paused to
reflect on the fact that this really great American is practically unknown to his fellow-countrymen. There are no
monuments to his memory in America. The tenants of the
premises he occupied in New York never heard of him.
His name is not mentioned in the local histories of his
birthplace. In the few brief references to him contained in
biographical dictionaries, the date of his birth is wrong.
The picture in the American Embassy at Tokyo which for
years was pointed out as that of Harris was not of him but
of Secretary of State Lewis Cass under whom he served.
Another picture of him which until a few weeks ago was
on file in the print room of the New York Public Library
was that of William E. Curtis, who, like Harris, had served
as President of the New York Board of Education. One of
the few genuine pictures of Harris ever published appears
as the frontispiece to this volume.

I might have lived and died without ever hearing his
name mentioned but for the fact that I was once a resident of Japan and became interested in the history of that
country. There Townsend Harris is appraised at his true
value. He is one of the heroes of the Japanese people and

they ungrudgingly admit a heavy debt of gratitude to him. If it were possible for any but a Japanese to be admitted to their pantheon of gods Harris would doubtless have been admitted years ago. They have done everything possible to make his memory sacred. The two places where he lived— the consulate at Shimoda and the legation at Tokyo—are marked and preserved as shrines. Every object he touched has been treasured as if it had been sanctified by contact with him.

Harris went to Japan at a time when he could be of the greatest possible service both to that country and to his own. Had some other man been given the difficult task to which he was assigned; had he been a man of different temperament; had any one of a number of conditions varied in the slightest degree, the history of Japan might have taken quite another course. It is idle to speculate on what that course might have been, but enough to say that under his guiding hand Japan was introduced into the family of nations under the most favorable possible conditions—favorable at the time not only for Japan but also for the rest of the world.

Harris was not an experienced diplomat; nor did he have the legal training which presumably would have been of help to him not only in the negotiation of agreements but in the writing of the text of conventions and treaties. He was not by any means a brilliant man. I doubt if he ever said anything clever in his life. His abilities were those of the patient and persevering student; his point of view toward problems of diplomacy was that of the New York merchant who was interested in foreign trade. The patience and perseverance which enabled him to master three foreign languages with the aid of dictionaries also enabled him to overcome the determined opposition and obstruction of the Japanese. Beset on every side by deception and evasion, he allowed nothing to swerve him from his course of sincerity and friendship, tactics which were as strange to the Japanese as theirs were to him.

But his previous experience in the East was helpful. As he had lived among the Chinese and the Malays and had become painfully well acquainted with the Siamese, he was able to meet the Japanese with the proper perspective. He was not blinded by their quaintness, nor was he unduly impressed by their emphasis on a strange and peculiar etiquette. In his life on the China Coast and his more recent experience in Siam he had met many strange people and the Japanese had no startling surprises for him. They were just another Oriental people—not exactly like the Chinese, Malays or Siamese, but bred in the same human rabbit warren—not to be looked upon as anthropological specimens but as human beings whose kinship to others of the race had been obscured by isolation.

Except for the prison-like residence of the Dutch on Deshima he was the first foreigner to live in Japan since the expulsion of the Catholic missionaries and he had no opportunity to learn about the people except through his own observations. Yet in a few weeks he had a better understanding of the character of the people than many later residents acquired after a residence of years. He soon learned of the simple honesty of the peasant which stood out in such sharp contrast to the studied deceit of the officials.

The treaty which he negotiated formed the basis of Japan's relations with the foreign powers during the most difficult period of Japanese history. It was entirely an individual achievement. Since the two names are inseparably linked in history it is impossible to avoid a comparison of

xiii

the resources and the achievements of Perry and Harris. The former had gone to Japan with a well-armed fleet, with interpreters, secretaries, a cargo of rich presents, several tons of coin for incidental expenses. Harris was landed on the inhospitable shore of the country, his status uncertain, without enough funds to meet his daily expenses. There he was forgotten by his government. He had no one to talk to but his Dutch interpreter. During a great part of the time he should have been in the hospital. He thought seriously of suicide. The mere fact that he kept alive was a triumph of will-power. The accomplishments of the two men have been aptly summed up by John W. Foster, a former Secretary of State:

"The genius of Perry had unbarred the gate of the island empire and left it ajar; but it was the skill of Harris which threw it open to the commercial enterprise of the world."*

He had hoped that his name would find an honorable place in the history of his country, but his countrymen have ignored his memory just as his government neglected him in his lifetime. It remained for a British historian to give an adequate summing up of his achievements:

The story of how, unbacked by any display of force under his country's flag, he succeeded by his own personal efforts in overcoming the traditional hatred of centuries to even the smallest association with foreigners, is one of marvelous tact and patience, of steady determination and courage, of straightforward uprightness in every respect, that is not exceeded by any in the entire history of the international relations of the world.†

That is the story this volume attempts to tell.

CARL CROW

* American Diplomacy in the Orient, by John W. Foster, The Riverside Press, Cambridge, 1904.
† Longford, J. H., *The Story of Old Japan.*

# ACKNOWLEDGMENT

THE writing of this book would not have been possible without the help of a great many people who have generously responded to my requests for assistance. It is not until I begin to list them in order to make grateful acknowledgment of my obligations that I realize to how many people—many of them unknown to me personally—I have written. It is a pleasure to be able to say that no one who could give me any help failed to do so.

At the head of the list of acknowledgments must come Dr. Mario Emilio Cosenza, Dean of Brooklyn College. In 1916 Dr. Cosenza became director of Townsend Harris Hall, the preparatory high school of the College of the City of New York, and his curiosity was aroused as to the life of the man after whom the school had been named. He was surprised to find that Harris was a man of genuine distinction and brilliant achievements of whom very few Americans had ever heard. The more he learned about the life of Harris the more interested he became and he studied and added to the collection of manuscripts and letters in the library of the College. It was through his efforts that "The Complete Journal of Townsend Harris" was published under the auspices of the Japan Society of New York. The value of this publication is multiplied many times by the very careful notes compiled by Dr. Cosenza, making it a complete source of information about the diplomatic career of Harris in Siam and Japan. Prior to the publication of the Journal by Dr. Cosenza the only attempt to present the life of Harris to his fellow-countrymen was made by Dr. W. E. Griffis, for many years a missionary in Japan and the author of a number of books about that country. His "Townsend Harris, First American Envoy to Japan" was published in 1895 and has long been out of print. It does not contain a complete journal and makes but passing reference to the work of Harris in Siam.

Among the many who have helped me with advice, suggestions, and research are:

Roland S. Morris, former American Ambassador to Japan

Nelson Trussler Johnson, American Ambassador to China

Cyril Wynne, Chief of the Bureau of Research and Publications, Department of State

G. V. Blue, of the same bureau

Whiteside Hill, Counsellor-at-Law, New York City

Miss Florence P. Spofford and Miss Maud Kay Sites of the Library of Congress

B. T. Townsend, Secretary of the Union Club, New York

Amasa W. Howland, Postmaster at Hudson Falls, New York

Sydney H. Coleman, Executive Vice-President of the American Society for the Prevention of Cruelty to Animals

Lyman Rhoades, New York City

Dr. Victor H. Paltsits, Keeper of Manuscripts, New York Public Library

Henry O. Severance, Honorary Consultant in Library
Practice, Library of Congress

H. M. Lyndenberg, New York Public Library

Mrs. William L. Wilson, New York City

Miles W. Vaughn and Glen Babb, formerly newspaper
correspondents in Tokyo

L. W. Jenkins, director of the East India Marine Hall,
Peabody Museum, Salem, Massachusetts

A. J. Gibney, Frank A. Munsey Co., New York

The research department of the Encyclopædia Britannica
has given me great assistance and I am also indebted to
the New York Public Library and to that model small library, the Scoville Memorial Library of Salisbury, Conn.
Both Miss Cherry Kennedy and Miss Lois Hike searched
through the court records of New York for the facts about
the business relationships of Townsend Harris and his
brother John, and J. Clinton Roraback of Canaan, Conn.,
helped me to interpret these musty old documents.

Finally I must not omit to mention the efficient and
helpful service of my niece, Miss Martha Lynn Beck, who
not only did a great deal of valuable research work for
me but typed the manuscript with its many revisions.

CARL CROW

## CHAPTER I

# THE BOY MERCHANT OF NEW YORK

SOMETIME during the year 1820 a freshly painted sign was to be seen over the doorway of the small brick building at 84 Pearl Street, a busy street in one of the most important retail districts of New York, announcing that this was the place of business of Townsend Harris, dealer in chinaware. Newly painted signs were going up almost every day in New York at that time, for the city had completely recovered from the British blockade of 1812 and was well started on a growth that had only momentarily been halted. But of the many new business establishments which marked its growing prosperity, none was more symbolic of the youthfulness of the city.

If Townsend Harris was not the youngest merchant whose name was listed in the current issue of the tiny city directory he was one of the youngest, for on October 4 of that year he celebrated his sixteenth birthday. At that early age he was not only a merchant but also the head of a household consisting of his adoring mother and a couple of orphan nieces who lived with him in the house next door to the chinaware shop. He was the man of the family. He managed his shop, supported his mother and looked after the education and culture of his nieces, sternly reprimanding them for wasting their time in reading what were considered to be the cheap and useless romances of the period.

Eight years before this time his older brother, John, had left the village of Sand Hill, a few miles south of Lake George, to make his fortune as a merchant in New York, the fastest-growing city in the country. New Yorkers were so sure of the future greatness of the place that they had just built a fine new City Hall which was admittedly much larger than demanded by the present needs of the city. It was a beautiful building and set an architectural standard for others to follow. Improvements were going on in all the occupied parts of the city, though much of it was still farm land. Hills were being leveled and swamps filled in the lower part of Manhattan. There was no doubt that both Boston and Philadelphia had lost in the contest for supremacy. One local enthusiast had actually made the prediction that in a hundred years the city would have a population of a million, might in fact become the largest city in the world.

The first trickle of immigration which was later to become a flood had started and Americans themselves were following new population trends. The grandsons of men who had pushed into the wilderness to settle on farms were now coming back to go into business in the big city. Brother John was one of these, for his Welsh ancestors had come to America with Roger Williams and the several generations of the family had never gotten very far away from the soil. But in spite of its promising future Brother John chose an unfortunate time to move to New York, for the growth of the city had been temporarily but effectively stopped by the second war with England and the British blockade which closed the port to all regular lines of business. Merchants were particularly hard hit, for there were no American factories of importance and they had to depend on England for their supplies. Those who were fortunate enough to have stocks of goods on hand sold them at good prices, but when their stocks were exhausted there was no way to replace them except at the high prices demanded by the blockade-runners and privateers. They were the only prosperous people in the city.

Brother John may have shared in this prosperity for his first place of business was at 83 Water Street, less than a hundred yards from the Old Slip where many of the privateers and blockade-runners docked.

The father of John and Townsend Harris had been the village hatter at Sand Hill but in 1812 the individual hatmakers were beginning to go out of business, for they could not meet the competition of Connecticut factory production at Danbury where several years previously a pioneer had inaugurated mass production by turning out four hats a day. Brother John came to the conclusion that it was not a business for his young generation and that Sand Hill was too restricted in the opportunities it offered. But his choice of the chinaware business was an unhappy one, for England was the only source of supply. However, he was a business man of more than the usual amount of initiative and daring even in that period when all Americans were poor and all were made daring by the conviction that they were destined to become wealthy. For the moment destiny was pursuing an erratic course. With the British blockade there were a good many failures and bankruptcies, and New York landlords for the first time in their experience found themselves with vacant buildings on their hands and no demand from tenants. The real estate depression affected all parts of the city, but property owners in the retail sec-

3

tion around Pearl and Wall and the neighboring streets were especially hard hit.

Brother John who had just arrived from the country did not share the pessimism of some of the older residents. He believed that this slump was only temporary, that New York real estate was bound to increase in value, and was willing to risk his limited capital on his judgment. But even at the low prevailing prices it took a good deal of money to finance the purchase of real estate while on the other hand landlords were eager to sign long leases with anyone who could pay the rent. So while he set himself up in the chinaware business at 83 Water Street, he leased a number of other places in the neighborhood including some property from Trinity Church, preparing to hold on to the leases until he could dispose of them at a profit. He did not have to wait long. With the lifting of the British blockade there was a boom in real estate and an urgent demand for business quarters. Brother John made some very handsome profits. He sold one lease to premises on Wall Street for $18,000 and also disposed of his lease on Trinity Church property for $14,000. There is no reason to believe that he lost money on any of his leases.

At the time the young brother Townsend was set up in business, all signs of the depression caused by the war had disappeared and the town was booming in the manner of Western towns of a few generations later. It had a population of 125,000 which was increasing so rapidly that it was doubled ten years later. It was well on its way to the population of a million which had been predicted. The streets above Canal were beginning to fill up with scattered houses. New York was somewhat surprised to find itself a metropolis and there was some delay and difficulty

4

about adjusting itself to city ways. Only a few years before, no less than 20,000 hogs had been running loose in the city.

With Brother John busy and prosperous the rest of the Harris family had moved to New York, and Townsend, the youngest of the three sons, went to work as clerk in a dry-goods store. In the meantime Brother John continued to expand and he had a good many irons in the fire. Cargoes of chinaware were arriving regularly from England and unloaded at the Old Slip which was separated only a few yards from his shop at 83 Water Street. He also maintained another office in Wall Street where he and a partner by the name of Chauncey continued to dabble in real estate. It didn't take him long to come to the conclusion that younger brother Townsend would be more valuable to himself and to the family as a partner than as an employee of another concern and so he set him up in business at the Pearl Street address, one of the many places he had leased when rentals were low. He had started in business at 83 Water Street but had sublet part of these premises and moved to offices on Wall Street probably because rentals were lower there. His Wall Street office was located just around the corner where he could easily keep an eye on the young merchant. The Water Street establishment now became a wholesale concern while the retail business was turned over to Townsend on Pearl Street. Brother John was the active head of the partnership but so far as the public was concerned there was nothing to indicate that Townsend was not an independent merchant.

The two brothers continued a family partnership in the chinaware business in this neighborhood for more than thirty years but with a number of removals—none of more than a few blocks, for they never went north of Wall Street.

During the first twenty years they maintained separate business establishments, one wholesale and the other retail, but the retail business was finally discontinued and the brothers occupied the same premises as wholesalers. In the meantime the district had been almost completely destroyed by the great fire of 1835 and Brother John was the only lucky tenant of the district. Of the 528 buildings in the fire area his premises at 83 Water Street alone escaped. "There it stood, unscathed, an oasis in the surrounding desert," wrote a local chronicler. Brother John must have thought this escape was significant. He had started in business at this address and after a number of moves he was back at the same narrow five-story building more than forty years later. In 1836 Townsend Harris was in business at 83 Pearl and his brother was almost directly across the street at 76 Pearl. They both lived at 426 Hudson which was then developing as a popular residence district leading from the business district around Trinity to Greenwich. Hudson was then surrounded by gardens and green fields and offered an unobstructed view of the river. Its scattered residences extended all the way up to Greenwich where the few local residents were patronizingly referred to as "villagers" by their metropolitan neighbors who lived in the southern portion of the island.

Townsend had barely come of age when he began real estate deals on his own account and appears to have made this a very profitable side line to his chinaware business, though he never operated on as large a scale as his brother. He bought two lots on Bleecker running north to Minetta, paying $10,500 for the property, and less than six weeks later sold the lots at a profit of $2,000. Later he purchased the house and lot at the corner of Charles and Hudson for $6,000 and before the end of the year sold it at a profit of $1,000.

Brother John was the business man of the family. Like many another boy of that period, Townsend was a merchant because it offered the most logical career open to an ambitious youngster whose education was confined to the three R's of "reading, 'riting, and 'rithmetic." Even to those who had an opportunity to train for them, the professions did not offer the golden rewards of later generations. The boys with educations became teachers, preachers, doctors, or lawyers. Few made fortunes and the few who gained fame were the lawyers who drifted into politics. Business of one sort or another was the one solid and thoroughly respectable occupation for any lad with abilities above those of the farm hand or the day laborer.

Had Townsend chosen a vocation for himself or had one been chosen for him by any one of the many scientific formulas now in vogue, it would certainly not have been a business career. There were doubtless a thousand other bright and energetic lads on the island of Manhattan who would have taken more pride than he did in the fact that his name appeared over a chinaware shop, for while he had been brought up in the Yankee trading tradition, he did not inherit the trading genius or the Yankee love for barter. He was interested in reading and the study of languages, had an artist's love of beauty in form and color. But hardheaded Brother John was a business man—a very successful one—and a business career was the only one that came within the scope of his imagination. In the long partnership of the two brothers, it was John who conceived the plans and made the decisions and Townsend who was his

7

willing and loyal and capable assistant. What he lacked in keen business instincts he made up for in charm of manner —an ability to make sales and to appease the most disgruntled customer. It was in many ways an ideal partnership.

Townsend had no time to go to school but he did have time to read and he was seldom without a book in his hand. There were many hours in his retail shop when there were no customers to serve and there were long evenings when he read books with his mother, talked over the affairs of the limited world they knew, and argued politics with her—there were plenty of opportunities for arguments. She was an ardent Tory who believed in keeping the lower classes in their place and saw nothing but cause for alarm in the changed and changing conditions of life in New York. To her mind Sand Hill had been a better place. He was a conscientious liberal and welcomed with the enthusiasm of youth the changes going on about him in this rapidly growing young country. It was only on the question of politics the two ever disagreed. The bond of affection between them was so strong that she was to him what many women are to most men. He never married and no other woman ever came into his life.*

His maturity did not change their relationship and up to the time of her death he clung to her like a timid and affectionate small boy. It is said that they were separated only twice, once when Townsend made a short business trip to Ohio and another time when he sent his mother and nieces to the Catskills to escape a cholera epidemic which was raging in New York. When the chinaware business grew to a point that it was necessary to make frequent business trips to London, it was always older brother John

* *Townsend Harris*, by Griffis.

who had to go because Townsend would not be separated from his mother.

Because of her he repressed a natural love of adventure and desire to travel and found his only release in the reading of books and the study of foreign languages. He was an omnivorous reader and though his choice was for serious books which were packed full of the strong intellectual meat of the day, he familiarized himself with strange scenes and foreign characters by reading the work of those popular new novelists, Thackeray and Bulwer-Lytton. He got so much enjoyment out of these books by English authors that he wondered what he might find in books written in other languages and in order to satisfy that curiosity he bought dictionaries and laboriously mastered French, Italian and Spanish. In studying these languages he was following the example of Benjamin Franklin, the middle-class hero of America, whom Harris and thousands of other young men sought to emulate.

The reading of these books made him a cosmopolitan although he never got outside New York City. His circle of friends was not confined to the merchants of Pearl, Water and Wall Streets. Though the term was then unknown outside of Russia, he belonged to the *intelligentsia*, but his tastes were catholic. He made friends of portrait painters, teachers, preachers, politicians, and the immigrants from Europe who came flocking to the city. His business also gave him a broader point of view than that of many of the local business men. As the chinaware which he sold was imported from England he learned about the intricacies of foreign trade. The American ships which were beginning to find their way to all ports of the world were built and docked in the neighborhood, and he saw many of them launched. He had only to walk around the corner from his shop to see the ships of many foreign flags which were docked in the neighborhood of the Battery. There were plenty of officers of sailing ships ready to talk to him in French or Spanish or Italian.

In spite of his bookishness and his devotion to his mother, Harris had time to devote to other things. He joined the militia and had as much fun as any of the other young men of New York at the annual celebration of "Evacuation Day," the anniversary of the date the British troops had sailed back to England. Though no records of his membership have been found he was doubtless a member of one of the many volunteer fire companies. As he grew older he took on the duties and dignities of maturity. He taught a Sunday School class, became an active member of the Chamber of Commerce and was given that final and convincing testimonial of personal integrity and financial soundness—an election as trustee of a savings bank. His conservative mother was probably shocked when he became one of the early members of Tammany and began taking an interest in the politics of his ward. New York politics was acquiring a new interest and offering new opportunities, for the franchise was being extended and the men qualified to vote were not only increasing in number but were being given more power. At the time Harris came of age there was a movement on foot to select a mayor by popular vote instead of accepting an appointee selected by the political machine at Albany. The change actually did come about later and in 1834 Cornelius W. Lawrence took his seat as the first mayor elected by the voters of the city.

But it was his interest in schools rather than in politics that made Harris active in Tammany's then limited affairs.

10

His own difficulties in securing an education for himself had given him ideas about public schools which for that day were strange and radical to the point of being revolutionary. He believed that the city should, at the expense of the taxpayers, provide a free college education for students who wanted to go beyond the primary grades where public education then began and ended. Even the primary schools were very poorly served, for there were said to be more than 25,000 children in New York who had never been to any kind of school.

When he had been a Tammany man long enough to ask favors of the organization and the political plums were being passed around, he asked for the sourest plum of the lot—a seat on the Board of Education which had few powers and no honors. The position gave him an opportunity to put into practice ideas that had been maturing in his mind for years. While other members took but a perfunctory interest in what was to them a minor political job, he found in it an opportunity for public service as well as the enjoyment of a hobby. All the energies and enthusiasms which the routine of his business career had suppressed found a release in this work. He was soon elected president of the board—a thankless office which no one else wanted but one in which he took inordinate pride. He used it to push through his pet project which was the establishment of a free academy for the children of New York.

His work on the Board of Education brought him into intimate contact with a class of men whom he would never have met in the chinaware shop. One of them was General Prosper M. Wetmore, one of the leading citizens of New York, who shared with him an enthusiastic interest in

11

popular education. He had served a term in the state legislature where he was chairman of the committee on colleges and academies and he had advocated a bill to establish school district libraries. Like Harris, Wetmore's education had been sketchy and was rounded out by his own efforts. On the death of his father he had been put to work in a counting house but at the age of thirty he had written a volume of poems which was published in New York. Another friend Harris made was the young lawyer, William H. Seward, whose eloquent speeches were the talk of the state. If they did not meet when Seward was studying law in New York they undoubtedly met later when Seward, as a member of the state legislature, was working for the improvement of the public schools of the state.

The proposal to establish a free academy was met at first either with indifference or with active opposition. The opposition came from sources that were powerful and influential, for it was led by the trustees of Columbia University who were jealous of the prestige of the only institution in the city devoted to higher education. The steady influx of Irish immigrants provided another objection for few saw any reason why the sons and daughters of these ignorant and poverty-stricken immigrants should be educated at the public expense. The fact that most of the Irish immigrants were Catholics did not add to the popularity of the movement.

Harris did not allow anything to divert or discourage him. He secured the support of men like General Wetmore who were in favor of free education, and the Tammany politicians endorsed the movement if for no other reason than that he was a good Tammany man and therefore

12

deserving of support. No doubt a great many of his opponents gave in solely because of his persistence.

He eventually carried the project through as he had planned it and is justly given credit for being the creator of what is now the College of the City of New York.

## CHAPTER II

## THE FAMILY BLACK SHEEP

O N THE celebration of his forty-third birthday Townsend Harris had every reason to be satisfied with
himself, for he was by all the generally accepted standards
of New York a very successful man. Though still young,
he had started in business so early that he had more than
a quarter of a century of successful business experience
behind him. He owned real estate and was trustee of a
savings bank. He was not wealthy but enjoyed a good,
solid, middle-class prosperity. His accomplishments in
foreign languages and his wide reading had given him a
culture that set him apart not only from business men
but also from most of the other residents of New York.
There were few men in the city with a wider or more
varied circle of friends. He was not especially happy in
the business world but he had first found release from its
drudgery in reading and a study of languages. Now he
had a far more satisfactory avocation, for he had succeeded
in his plans for the establishment of a free academy for
New York and as president of the Board of Education
he would have every opportunity to foster the growth of
this pet project.

Less than two years later he was branded by his elder
brother as the family black sheep, and like a small boy
who is humiliated at the discovery of his guilt, ran away
to sea.

Townsend Harris at the time he was president of the Board of Education of New York

*From a bronze tablet by Albert P. D'Andrea, of the Art Department of the Townsend Harris Hall High School*

The four classes of society in Japan — soldier, farmer, laborer, merchant

*From a native drawing*

While there may have been other reasons, the immediate cause of this great change appears to have been the death of his mother at the age of 83. Her death affected him not only as the death of a mother would affect a devoted son but also as the death of a sweetheart would have affected a romantic young man. The balance wheel of his life was gone—the incentive to accomplishment which would bring the approval of his mother. He began drinking steadily and intemperately and although his friends insisted that he never drank to such an extent as to be incapacitated for business, they admitted that he was usually noticeably under the influence of liquor in the afternoons when all respectable business men were cold sober and clear headed.* There was plenty of temptation at hand for one who was inclined to tipple at unconventional hours. A bottle was handily at his elbow, for he had sublet a part of the chinaware shop to a firm of grocers who as a convenience to their customers and visitors maintained a small private bar where drinks were free to all callers. And Harris was just the sort of man anyone would enjoy having a drink with.

After more than a quarter of a century of careful attention to business he began to neglect it and for the first time since it had been founded the partnership of the Harris brothers began to show a decrease in the volume of sales. Old customers had drinks with the junior partner but placed their orders elsewhere. Previously the business had been so prosperous and had appeared to be so sound that Brother John, who was getting on in years, had practically retired and had established himself comfortably in London where he looked after the purchase

* See letter of Nathaniel Dougherty in State Department files.

of stock while Townsend attended to the sales in New York. Brother John was greatly upset by reports of the dwindling profits which even turned to losses and immediately jumped to the conclusion that this was due to the fact that Brother Townsend was devoting too much time to the affairs of the Board of Education, a project for which he had no enthusiasm. He wrote him a strong elder-brotherly letter on the subject—a letter so full of reproaches and charges of disloyalty and ingratitude that Townsend reluctantly resigned from the Board.

But instead of helping matters this only made them worse. The work of getting the new free academy organized and started on a successful career had helped him to forget his grief over the death of his mother, but now that he was thrown back to the tedium of the chinaware business, he drank even more. Perhaps it was not entirely his fault that the business was no longer prosperous. Demand for chinaware had not grown as fast as competition. When Brother John had started the business he had only a few competitors but now there were fifteen chinaware importers on Water Street alone and almost a hundred in a radius of a few blocks. It was a business which attracted many because the goods did not become shopworn or unsaleable through fashion changes. Exasperated Brother John received further reports of shrinking profit and actual losses and finally wrote demanding that the partnership be dissolved. He would come back from London, take over the business, and run it himself.

 This was a final blow to Townsend. He had lost his mother, his reputation, had abandoned his career as an educator and had now been branded by his elder brother as the black sheep of a hitherto wholly respectable family. He did not wait for Brother John's return to New York and the recriminations he would have to listen to, but made some hasty financial arrangements, bought a half-interest in a sailing-ship and started on a trading expedition to the Far East. No doubt he discussed these plans with his friend General Wetmore who was then Secretary of the New York Chamber of Commerce and was interested in a shipping venture in Nicaragua. When the next issue of the growing but still diminutive volume which comprised the New York city directory appeared, the notation opposite his name read "gone to San Francisco." In the following issue his name was omitted.

He sailed from New York in May 1849, on the long route around the Horn to San Francisco, and there became the sole owner of the ship and the trading enterprise. Possibly his new partner remained to try his luck in gold mining as did many others who touched the port of San Francisco during that hectic gold rush period. There must have been considerable delay in San Francisco or possibly, before he continued to the China Coast, Harris made a trip to the Puget Sound region to secure a cargo of furs for sale in Canton, for he was still in the North Pacific on Christmas Day of that year. Little is known of his life in the Far East except that he was in Manila for Christmas the following year (1850), and in Penang the next year. Like most other American merchant-sailors of that period he did not depend on round trip voyages to the home port, and the regular import and export trade, but sailed about from port to port either buying cargo in one place to sell in another or carrying freight for other merchants. Many of these early American traders sailed away from New York, Salem or Boston and did not return for years. They bought rice in Siam, sugar in Manila or furs on the northwest coast, all for sale in Canton. A few had made very handsome profits shipping cargoes of ice to Canton and Calcutta from the frozen shore of Vladivostok.

At first Harris prospered but he made some unlucky ventures in what was at best a very hazardous business and in about two years was compelled to sell the ship. The new owner brought the vessel back to New York. Here Brother John hunted up the captain who had sailed with Townsend and in the presence of a witness made anxious inquiries about the conduct of the younger brother. (He had not heard the details of Townsend's drinking until his return to New York, when he wrote another elder-brotherly letter, full of grief and indignation. To this Townsend replied reassuringly that he had already reformed and would never again fall into bad habits. But Brother John quite reasonably refused to place faith in the promises of a man who would lead an upright and abstemious life until well past forty and then suddenly become dissipated. Hence his inquiries to the captain.) The captain assured the elder brother that in the two years they had been on the ship together he had never seen Townsend intoxicated. Those who are inclined to be skeptical might note that he did not say he had never seen him take a drink, and the term "intoxicated" as used by a sailing-ship captain of that period was one which allowed a great deal of latitude. But there is no evidence that Harris ever made a further contribution to the reputation for drunkenness which he had already acquired.

There are no records as to what Harris did after losing ownership of his ship except that he established a residence in Hongkong where he boarded with the Drinkers, a well-known American family. Captain Drinker was one of the pioneer American merchants in this new British colony. In a journal which he began to keep several years later Harris records the fact that he spent Christmas of 1851 in Penang and the three successive years in Singapore, Hongkong and Calcutta. In other places he mentions visits to Ceylon, trips through the jungles of Java and extensive tours of North China. He must have traveled even farther afield than his journal indicates, for in his later years he told of experiences with the head-hunters and cannibals of the South Seas. He made seven visits to Penang and also visited Burma, India, Borneo and Siam.

In all of these places he made friends of the type and class of General Wetmore and of Seward, who by this time had become the leader of the Whig party in New York and had hopes of becoming President. Among his friends was Sir John Bowring, the learned governor of Hongkong, and the two appear to have found many interests in common. In his travels he naturally met the American Consuls at all of the ports as well as Consuls and merchants of other nationalities, and soon he had scattered about the ports of the Far East a collection of friends even more mixed than those whose companionship he had enjoyed in New York. There his knowledge of languages had been an ornamental but useless accomplishment. Here in this polyglot community it opened the door to many new and interesting friendships. He soon became an amateur diplomat as did every foreign resident of the China Coast. Shanghai and other ports of China had just been opened to the foreigner and complicated trade and diplomatic arrangements between China and the foreign powers were being built up. The subject of treaty rights was on the tip of everyone's tongue and was talked about just as local politics was talked at home. Here one came in contact with all the powers having interests or ambitions in China and learned of their policies at first hand. Every club and every tea table on the China Coast, then as now, provided a forum for the discussion of international politics.

There was probably no great difficulty about Harris' getting occasional employment on business errands to different parts of the Far East, for dependable super-cargoes were always in demand and he was far above the average both in character, experience and ability. His knowledge of languages provided a very valuable and useful equipment and he had now mastered a new one, Malay. He probably did make some business trips out of Hongkong, but the fragmentary record of his journeys suggests the leisurely travel of the adventurous student rather than the hurried trips of the business man. Even today the man on a business trip does not often visit Agra, Lucknow or the Taj Mahal, the Tomb of Akbar, and these places then were much more remote and inaccessible than at present.

After leaving the rustic simplicity of Sand Hill, Harris had spent the next thirty years of his life in Lower Manhattan, reading about many strange and interesting places but seeing none of them. Sailing-ships of the seven seas had docked and discharged cargo in sight of his Water Street office—whetting his appetite for travel and adventure. Now when these long-delayed opportunities came, he plunged into them and enjoyed them like an intelligently adventurous youth on his first journey into a strange land. In the numerous references he made to his visits to these places there is no hint as to the business which called him there but pages of observation about animals and plants and the beauties of nature. Like most self-educated men he had an intelligent interest in all manner of things. And like many another lover of nature he always regretted that he had not studied botany and was constantly ashamed of his inability to give the correct names of the flowers and trees that he saw. But his lack of botanical knowledge did not prevent his describing with considerable accuracy the various manifestations of vegetable life which he observed. His interest in nature went even farther than that, for he made careful inquiries about snakes in seven different countries and was mildly wrathful at the exaggerations of travelers who wrote of having seen boa constrictors more than thirty feet long. He was as intelligently and methodically curious as his hero, Franklin. At several places in the tropics he noted the brilliant and puzzling display of fireflies where hundreds of them on the same small tree will flash on and off in unison as if all were controlled by one electric switch. He timed the flashes and made a rough calculation that they had the same frequency as the normal pulse beat.

He was an insatiable sight-seer but it was beauty rather than the curious or the spectacular that interested him. Having once seen the fascinating ugliness of Aden he had no desire to make a second visit. Having seen the Pyramids of Egypt emerge from darkness in the light of the rising sun he recorded his regret that he later visited them in the garish noonday sunlight. His love of beauty made him an early riser. He got up at five o'clock in the morning to visit a temple and admire the brilliancy and blue tinge of

Sirius, the dog star, as seen in India and Egypt, where it shines more brightly than Venus as seen in the United States.

The tropical beauty of Penang stirred his heart as it has stirred the heart of every artist who ever visited the place. Its lush tropical vegetation and eternal springtime must have made a very deep impression on one who had spent so many years surrounded by the bricks and paving stone of lower New York. One of the longest entries in his journal contains a detailed description of a thunder squall as seen from the Penang Hills:

Up at daylight to see the beautiful changes of light and shade produced by the rising sun; indeed it is a constant source of enjoyment to watch the effect of those changes during the day; now, the light cloud passing quickly over the sun, seems to race down the mountain, across the plain, across the water over to the Province Wellesly; where now it darkens for a moment the golden paddy fields—next seems to deepen the green of the canes growing on the various sugar estates. Next dark masses of cloud rise up over Elephant Mountain. The leaden colour of its advanced edge does not leave you in doubt for a moment as to its nature—it is a thunder squall. Soon the vivid lightning begins to dart about—next you hear a faint mutter of thunder; the cloud hurries on; the lightning plays incessantly; the crash of the thunder is distinct; you see the curtain formed by the falling rain, down to the tops of the palm trees at a distance of twenty miles—on it comes—now the tall white chimneys of the sugar boiling houses are shut out—now it strikes the shipping—the town—the plain—the palm trees and houses are shut out from view. You hear a low sound like an angry roar and it has reached the hilltop. You are in the cloud itself. What blinding lightning—the roll of the thunder never ceases. It continues half an hour, an hour or three hours, and then the clouds roll away to the southeast and the sun comes out once more. In all parts of the tropics the thunder is heavy and the lightning vivid, but I never saw such grand displays of God's pyrotechnics as in Penang.

These are not the comments of the business man who has the worries of an unsold cargo or an unsatisfactory agency arrangement. There is no evidence and no suggestion that any of his many trips were made for business purposes. On the other hand there is good reason to believe that for some years after the loss of his ship Harris was not compelled to earn a living but led a leisurely life and traveled a great deal merely for the pleasure of traveling. It was possible to do this in the Far East on a very small income, and a man of his accomplishments and personal charm would find a welcome everywhere. He was one of the best-known and most popular Americans on the China Coast. Perhaps he did not sink all his money in the sailing-ship venture or perhaps he was one of the numerous "remittance men" who have always been numbered among the foreign residents of the China Coast. The anger and disappointment of Brother John must have softened with the passage of the years. When he died in 1853 the account books showed a large amount of money due from Townsend, but the latter denied that he owed anything.

CHAPTER III

## BEGINNING LIFE AT FIFTY

O N HIS voyage from San Francisco to the China Coast
Harris skirted the shores of Japan and like every
other traveler wondered what lay beyond the terraced and
wooded shores in that mysterious group of beautiful islands
from which foreigners were so rigorously excluded. Except
for the Dutch who were allowed to bring in one ship a
year and were confined to the small island of Deshima in
the harbor of Nagasaki and Chinese who suffered similar
restrictions, no foreigners were allowed to visit Japan; and
the mystery with which the country was surrounded had
led to the growth of the most fantastic tales of fabulous
wealth, as signified by stories of temples roofed with solid
gold. He had visited every other country in the Far East and
when the Perry Expedition to Japan was announced he
thought this might provide him with the opportunity to
visit this strange country, the goal of every adventurous
traveler. The commodore anchored at Shanghai on May
4, 1853, on his way to Japan and Harris approached him
with an offer of his services which were politely but firmly
declined. He was only one of thousands from all parts of
the world, including many famous scientists, who had
similar ambitions and whose applications had been rejected.

Perry took the practical and common-sense attitude that
if he allowed a single civilian to join the expedition there

24

would be many more with equal claims to consideration; therefore he solved the problem by refusing all (with one exception) and confined the personnel of the expedition to the naval offices and the necessary interpreters. In order to protect himself against the pleas, importunities, and political influence to which he might be subjected, he made this the subject of his Second General Order, which he issued at sea on December 23, 1852. The one exception was the young journalist and poet, Bayard Taylor, who joined him at Shanghai in a capacity which may be best described as "ghost writer." Perry did not permit Taylor to publish anything he wrote, but liberal use was made of his journal in the voluminous official report of the expedition.

It would be interesting to know on what grounds Harris justified his request to accompany the expedition and in what capacity he proposed to serve. He had never been to Japan and his knowledge of the country was only the jumble of information and misinformation which he would have picked up on the China Coast. He had had no diplomatic experience and his knowledge of languages was of no value because Dutch was the only foreign language with which the Japanese were familiar. But among the hundreds of men Perry met in the Far East, Harris was one of the very few who appear to have made a lasting impression.

The visit of Perry apparently made an equally powerful impression on Harris for this dramatic enterprise called his attention to his own rather aimless life. He had had an opportunity to achieve a certain local fame as the president of the Board of Education of New York and the founder of the city's first free academy, but among many men in New York he was known only as a tippler and a business failure. Now he was drifting indolently toward the obscurity of an undistinguished life on the China Coast. There may have been another reason for his suddenly revived energy. Whatever news he received from Brother John could not have been reassuring, for John was on his deathbed and when he died in the winter of that year it was found that his once prosperous business had fallen on such evil days that the assets, some of which were of doubtful value, exceeded the liabilities by less than $300. If Townsend had been drawing semi-charitable profits from this business, they could not be continued. He would have to make his own living.

The one logical, though poorly paid, career which seemed open to him was the consular service of his own country at some port on the China Coast. He had good reason to believe that he could get a modest post of this sort. All governmental appointments were made as a reward for political services. In fact W. L. Marcy, who was serving as Secretary of State, was the author of that famous political creed "to the victors belong the spoils." The Democrats were still in power and Harris had been a good Tammany man, still had friends who would use their influence for him. And he knew that he was far better equipped for a consular position than many of those who represented American interests in the Far East.

After Perry's refusal to take him on the expedition to Japan he wrote a letter to the Secretary of State applying for a consular appointment either at Canton or at Hongkong. These were the only important consular offices on the China Coast for Shanghai had been open to trade only a few years and the duties of Consul were so unimportant that they were carried out by one of the local American merchants. The princely American firm of Russell & Co. was at that time the biggest business organization in the Far East and the manager of the Shanghai branch of the company acted as American Consul. Harris wrote to his old Tammany associates and also to his old friend General Wetmore to enlist their support and they brought influence to bear on the State Department. General Wetmore was especially active in his behalf and in a letter to Secretary Marcy said he had never met the superior of Harris "in a thoroughly educated and accomplished merchant," adding that he thought "from his unusually extensive acquirements on all commercial subjects and his acquaintance with several foreign languages (such as Spanish, French, Italian) that he could not fail to render himself useful in a consular office." But there were deserving Democrats in office at both Hongkong and Canton and no vacancies.

It was not until more than a year after he sent his application that a vacancy did occur, but not in a post for which he had applied. On August 2, 1854, he was appointed Consul to Ningpo. This had formerly been a rather important post but with the opening of Shanghai as a port, the shipping at Ningpo had dwindled and the fees which he collected and was allowed to retain were no longer sufficient to support the Consul. The appointment of Harris to this unattractive post had been made possible by the transfer of Consul Bradley to the more lucrative position of Consul at Singapore. The office of Consul at Ningpo did not provide any salary, for the State Department, then as now, was successful in its efforts to make the diplomatic work of the government self-supporting. The Consul also acted as consular judge for which he received an annual salary of $1000; the only other compensation came from fees, the principal source being the entering and clearing of American merchant vessels. As more and more shipping was being diverted to the growing port of Shanghai the fees of the Ningpo Consulate grew smaller in volume until Consul Bradley could no longer meet his living expenses and so was transferred.

In the meantime the Perry expedition had paid its first and second visit to Japan, the barriers of centuries of exclusion had been broken down. The treaty which allowed American ships to buy provisions at Shimoda and Hakodate, two of the most inadequate ports in Japan, had been ratified and the ratifications exchanged. Fortunes were being made out of the gold fields of California and it was believed by many that other fortunes would be made in trade with Japan if the door which had been pushed ajar by Perry could be thrown open. Letters which Harris received from his friends in New York gave him new and larger ambitions which made even the posts at Hongkong or Canton unattractive. They had discovered that there would be less competition for the appointment as Consul-General to Japan than to any other of the thousands of appointments which the President was empowered to make. When they reluctantly agreed to the treaty provisions for the residence of a consular representative, the Japanese officials were very insistent in their statements to Commodore Perry that they "wanted no women in Shimoda." President Pierce was obligated to respect their wishes and appoint a bachelor, and of the good Democratic bachelors, Harris was undoubtedly the most worthy and most suitable.

He did not wait in Hongkong to hear about the fate of

his application but determined to return home at once and make a personal appeal to secure the new and more important post of Consul-General to Japan. It was the first burst of energy and evidence of determination he had shown since he bought half-interest in the sailing-ship.

He was in Penang en route to New York visiting his old bachelor friend, Consul Currier, when he received official notification of his Ningpo appointment which was no longer of any interest to him. Before sailing from Penang, he wrote letters to a Baptist missionary living in Ningpo, appointing him as Vice-Consul and giving him authority to carry on with the duties of the office. But he did not entirely escape the unwelcome appointment because for years afterwards the missionary bombarded him with letters of complaint about the hard work and poor pay of the office and begged for some consular post in Japan. The unimportance of the Ningpo office is shown by the fact that from the time of the Harris appointment until the consulate there was abolished, the office of Consul was filled by some American missionary who combined evangelism with his consular duties.

Having taken care of this business, written a number of personal letters to friends in Hongkong and, apparently, borrowed some money from his old friend and host, Consul Currier, he sailed from Penang on May 21, 1855 by way of the overland Suez route. He made a remarkably fast trip for that period, for he was in New York in a little more than two months.

He had planned to make a visit to Paris but on his arrival in London he found important letters from General Wetmore and others which caused him to hurry on to New York. A few months before this, President Pierce had attempted to fill the Japanese post by offering it to the historian John Romeyn Brodhead, a man seemingly well-fitted for the position. His historical researches in Holland had given him a certain familiarity with the Dutch language which would have been very useful in Japan and he had also a background of diplomatic experience: at the age of thirty, he had served as Secretary of Legation in London where Mr. Bancroft was then minister. But he declined the appointment to Japan and so General Wetmore renewed his efforts on behalf of Harris. Other friends came to the support of the prodigal returning from his long exile in the East.

In spite of the traditional hunger of politicians for any job that happens to be open, there do not appear to have been many applicants for the Japan post, which in many ways was a most unattractive one. It could only have been attractive to those ignorant of the conditions under which they would have to live in Japan. Those familiar with the Far East knew that life there would be marked by isolation and hardship. Actually it turned out to be very much worse in practice than it was in prospect. The glamor had begun and ended with the expensive Perry Expedition. The commodore had gone to Japan under the lavish protection of the American navy which has never had to count its pennies like the State Department. On his second visit he had been accompanied by ten men-of-war and a personnel of more than two thousand men. He had guards of honor, secretaries and interpreters, butchers and cooks, and the holds of his ships were loaded with provisions. The Consul-General would be isolated at the little fishing village of Shimoda, uncertain of his reception, with no de-

Commodore Perry's call on the Imperial Japanese Commissioners at Yokohama

One of the first results of the residence of foreigners in Japan was the invention of the jin-ric-sha by an American missionary

pendable source of supplies and with no one to protect him in case of difficulties.

But it was not all clear sailing so far as the appointment of Harris was concerned. Someone dug up the old story about his drunkenness and charges were filed at the State Department. These were brought to the attention of General Wetmore, and he sought for a vindication from Nathaniel Dougherty who had been a clerk in the Harris store. But instead of vindicating Harris, honest Dougherty told the truth, much as he disliked saying anything that would injure his old friend and employer for whom he had a manly affection. In a written reply to Wetmore, Dougherty told of the letter from Brother John which had caused Harris to resign from the Board of Education and added:

Shortly after this I noticed that occasionally in the afternoon he would be under the influence of liquor, which unfortunately was kept by our co-tenants *free* for their friends' use; but I wish you clearly to understand that I never saw him in such a state as to incapacitate him from business.

Mr. Dougherty, afraid that in his truth-telling he had prejudiced the chances of his old friend, added that he thought "his infatuation was but temporary." This letter was written on March 24, 1855, and General Wetmore sent it to Secretary Marcy the same day.

It appears that General Wetmore had succeeded in satisfying Secretary Marcy on this and all other points regarding the appointment of Harris and that President Pierce had come to a decision even before he met the applicant, that in fact the appointment was as good as made when Harris was in London. But something which has not been

31

disclosed caused the President to change his mind. However, he returned to his original decision. In a letter to Wetmore, Secretary Marcy quoted from a letter he had received from the President in which the latter wrote: "I shall appoint him at once and I think he had better sail as soon as possible."

Whether or not they knew of the decision of the President, the friends of Harris took no chances but pulled all the political strings they could lay their hands on. Within a few days after he landed on American soil eight prominent men of New York had signed a joint letter to President Pierce strongly recommending Harris for appointment to some diplomatic or consular post in the East. The letter did not mention the appointment to Japan and was couched in general terms so that if one appointment fell through some other might be considered. Apparently Harris had made up his mind to get an official appointment of some sort in the Far East, and while his heart was set on the Japanese post he would not have refused any other consular position on which he could support himself. One of the signers of this letter was the historian, Brodhead, who had refused the appointment to Japan only a few months previously. A supplementary letter from John J. Cisco, who was one of the eight signers of the first letter, also made no reference to any specific post but told of Harris' business career and in the concluding paragraph said: "As a politician he was a sound and reliable and influential Democrat, and I have reason to know that his views have undergone no changes; that he is a true Democrat now as ever before. I give this testimony with much pleasure."

Years later Harris learned that his application had also

32

been supported by Senator Seward and Commodore Perry. Seward was the bitter political apponent of Secretary Marcy but as senator from New York would have something to say about the appointment of a constituent. Perry had apparently remembered very distinctly the interview with Harris in Shanghai.

As soon as his ship docked Harris had a hasty conference with his friends and hurried on to Washington where he not only had several conferences with President Pierce, but dined with him. Harris was probably ill at ease on his first interview, for the American who returns home after some years in the East always feels himself in very strange surroundings. But the two men were much alike in character and temperament and soon got on well together. After the second interview the President wrote the letter to Marcy stating that his decision had been made, but for some curious and inexplicable reason kept Harris waiting. On August 4, Harris, still uncertain and anxious, wrote the President as follows:

Sir:

In consequence of letters which reached me last evening, I have postponed my return to New York and remain at this hotel, anxiously awaiting Your Excellency's decision on my application.

I have told Your Excellency that I have long had a strong desire to visit Japan; and so deep has this feeling become that, if I was offered the choice between Commissioner to China or Consul to Japan, I should instantly take the latter.

I have a perfect knowledge of the social banishment I must endure while in Japan, and the mental isolation in which I must live, and am prepared to meet it. I am a single man, without any ties to cause me to look anxiously to my old home, or to become impatient in my new one:—You may rely, Sir, that I will not ask for leave to visit my friends, or resign the place for any reasons of dislike of the country, but will devote myself, zealously, to the faithful discharge of my duties.

I have only to add, that I shall be much obliged by your early decision on my application.

Perhaps President Pierce was waiting for a pledge of this kind for on the same day the letter was written, he signed the commission of Townsend Harris as the first Consul-General to Japan. While Harris was still busy with preparations for this mission, he was given an important diplomatic errand to perform on his way to his new post—the negotiation of a commercial treaty with Siam.

## CHAPTER IV

# THE CONSUL-GENERAL FOR JAPAN

WHEN Townsend Harris sailed from Penang on the visit home which he hoped would result in his securing appointment as the first Consul-General to Japan he was conscious of his own lack of training for any but the routine of a Consul's clerkly duties. His experience as an importer and his brief career as the owner of a trading-ship had made him familiar with the formalities of consular invoices and the routine of entering and clearing ships in strange ports; he knew about tonnage dues and manifests and all other details of maritime procedure. No clerkly Vice-Consul could know them any better.

But he also knew that if he were made Consul-General to Japan he would be faced with more serious and more difficult duties in the form of diplomatic negotiations with the local and national officials, and he set about training himself for this possible task as resolutely as he had, in his youth, set about learning foreign languages with the aid of a dictionary. It is not easy, at the age of fifty, to form new habits of industry but he did—most successfully. In order to prepare himself for the work he hoped to do, and to establish the orderly and careful habits of a professional diplomat, he began keeping a journal, entering in it a concise account of the events of each day, the names of people he met, a list of letters received and dispatched. The journal, with a few gaps, contains daily entries from the time he left Penang until he reached home. Then the busy August and September he had spent in New York and Washington were summarized in one brief paragraph:

I omit the details of what I did in the United States, merely noting that on the 4th of August I was appointed Consul-General for Japan. During the same month the President was pleased to entrust me with the making of a commercial treaty with the kingdom of Siam, a matter in which Mr. Balestier was unsuccessful in 1851.

It can well be supposed that the months following his appointment were such busy ones that he had no time to record the events of the day and that what little spare time he had was spent in renewing old friendships. In addition to discussing the problems of Siam and Japan with President Pierce and Secretary Marcy, he had to learn the routine of State Department procedure for there would not be in Japan, as in the American Consulates in other parts of the world, any old employees familiar with departmental red tape. An interpreter had to be employed, for the only foreign language the Japanese spoke was a corrupt *pidgin* Dutch which they had picked up from the Dutch sailors at Nagasaki. He could not find a native-born American who spoke Dutch so employed Mr. Heusken, who was born in Amsterdam but had become a naturalized American citizen. Arrangements had also to be made with the navy to transport the new Consul-General to his post and see him safely settled. Stores and supplies had also to be provided for a long stay in a country where it would not be possible to purchase so much as a side of bacon or a pair of socks. He had to outfit himself as carefully as if he were going to spend several years on a desert island. Many people had to be consulted, including Commodore Perry who gave him brief but valuable advice as to how he should establish himself when he took up his residence in Japan.

In the midst of these preparations he was given heavy new responsibilities, for with the penuriousness which was characteristic of the State Department it was suddenly decided to accomplish two diplomatic jobs at the expense of one voyage. Secretary Marcy wrote Harris that on his way to Japan he was to stop over in Siam and attempt to negotiate a new commercial treaty with that country. The only treaty America had with Siam was the one made by Roberts twenty years previously. It had proven to be a most unsatisfactory and completely useless document for, only a few months after it was signed, the Siamese had nullified its provisions for free trade by the establishment of a series of trade monopolies held by the Siamese nobles at great profit to themselves.

In an attempt to open Siam to American trade Mr. Balestier, the Consul at Singapore, had been sent to Bangkok to negotiate a new treaty, but the reactionary party which was in power in Siam had taken advantage of his ignorance of Oriental etiquette to put him in a ridiculous position. And when the American envoy found that he had been made the laughing-stock of all Siam he blew up in a rage so glorious that it assumed historic proportions and foreign residents as well as the Siamese talked about it for years afterward. He not only accomplished nothing but made the Siamese more determined than ever to have nothing to do with diplomats from foreign countries.

At the time Harris was given this appointment America had no trade with Siam and the only permanent American residents were missionaries. Some of the missionaries had been living there for more than twenty years with no well-defined legal status and subject to the whims and caprices of the Siamese rulers. The fact that they could not purchase land on which to build churches, mission schools and hospitals had been the cause of frequent representations to the State Department. The files were full of correspondence on this subject.

There were also vague ideas that a big and profitable trade might be built up in the country and that with two new rulers on the twin thrones the country was ready for an epoch of progress and the adoption of Western ideas. On his way to Japan Commodore Perry had met the junior King of Siam whose hobby at the moment was an interest in ships and this had made a profound impression on the commodore. He had thought of making a treaty with Siam himself but had been diverted by other matters. However, in his enthusiasm over the possibilities of trade with Siam Secretary Marcy did not forget the government's obligations to the missionaries. Harris was specifically instructed to secure for them the right to pursue their work unmolested but was cautioned not to go too far in pressing for their interests in Japan, for Christianity was proscribed in that country.

The Siamese problems had been on the agenda of the State Department for many years with no sustained effort to solve them. One reason for Secretary Marcy's sudden decision in the matter was that he had received news of the British Treaty with Siam which had been negotiated by Sir John Bowring the preceding April. For some obscure reason he wanted the visit of Harris kept secret, for in a personal postscript to his official letter of instructions he wrote: "I advise that nothing should be said about the Siam negotiation. If it should become public, obstacles may be thrown in the way of it."

At this late date it is difficult to understand either why the project should have been kept secret or how secrecy could have been possible when a gunboat was being outfitted for the journey. In spite of this caution, Harris could not resist the impulse to advise his friend, Captain Drinker in Hongkong, of his new honor. He wrote less than ten days after receiving the appointment but apparently someone else had been in even more haste to impart this highly confidential information, for by the time the letter reached Captain Drinker he knew all about it and wrote Harris that his injunction as to secrecy was "rather amusing." It appears that several people had sent the same news and it was common knowledge up and down the China Coast.

A showy and bulky but obviously inexpensive lot of presents was bought for the rulers of Siam, following the diplomatic formula of the day that Oriental potentates should be frightened by gunboats and then mollified by gifts. The list provided for the first King included huge gilt mirrors, chandeliers, microscopes, rifles, pistols, revolvers, portraits of General Washington and President Pierce, and a large assortment of pictures and books. The second King was said to be interested in science and the gifts to him included all the useless but amusing electrical gadgets of the day, two being described as follows:

Electrical Sportsman: some feathers attached to small strings are fastened to a Leyden jar, the electricity causes them to fly in the air, the discharge of electricity from the sportsman gun causes them to drop as if shot.

A thunder house, to illustrate the effects of lightning on a

39

house if struck by it, and to show the use of the lightning rod in buildings.

These electrical toys were so numerous that all the letters of the alphabet were exhausted in listing them. No presents were provided for Harris to use in Japan, for the gifts Perry had left were considered sufficient for that country.

The arrangements were that the steam frigate *San Jacinto* would be stocked with provisions for Harris' long stay in Japan, the cargo of presents put on board and the ship proceed around the Cape of Good Hope to Penang where Harris would join it after a journey which would take him to London and Paris and then to the Red Sea gateway to the Far East by the overland Suez route. With all of these detailed arrangements to be taken care of, it appears that nothing was said about the compensation for his work in Siam; for it was the subject of correspondence several years later. His salary as Consul-General to Japan was to begin when he arrived in Shimoda and assumed his consular duties.

As the *San Jacinto* was going on a diplomatic mission, it was considered essential that it be surrounded by all possible pomp and circumstance which would impress the natives, and Captain Bell requested permission to recruit a band and purchase the necessary musical instruments. The Perry expedition had set the precedent for this, for his ships were accompanied by enough bands for a circus parade. Officials of the Navy Department finally granted Captain Bell's request with the provision that the instruments be paid for out of the "slush fund," which was accumulated by savings and salvage from the crew's rations and was in theory reserved to the use of the crew, for their benefit and amusement. This was, according to one of the officers of the *San Jacinto*, the first time the government had raided the "slush fund" and many and bitter were the arguments in the forecastle.

Harris hurried through his arrangements and on October 15 sailed for Liverpool on the steamer *Pacific* which New York newspapers a few years previously had hailed as "the largest steamer in the world" and the "monarch of the ocean." He says in his journal: "For reasons that I will omit, the voyage was the most unpleasant I ever made" and then refers to a very bad cold which he contracted a few days out of Liverpool "from unavoidable exposure." The future monarch of the ocean made the voyage in eleven days, which was considered to be a very creditable performance.

In London he called on Ambassador Buchanan who was later, as President, to receive the visit of the first Japanese embassy to America. There were a few other necessary calls when he hurried on to Paris where he spent almost a month. The great exhibition was on, the city crowded, and it was with great difficulty that he got a room which he could only reach by climbing 132 steps.

On his arrival in Paris the first thing he attended to was the purchase of a wardrobe including, as he says in his journal, "some properly ornamented clothes to wear at the court of Bangkok." This was, in fact, the only indispensable errand he had to attend to on his long trip from New York to Penang. There were more than a thousand tailors in New York but with his fastidious ideas about dress, the tailors of Paris were the only ones skillful enough to provide those ceremonial garments. According to one of his biographers he had so conscientiously followed his grand-

41

mother's advice to "fear God, tell the truth and hate the British" that he would never buy a Sheffield knife or wear an article of clothing of British manufacture. There is good reason to doubt this statement, for whatever prejudices he may have had in his youth must have been softened or destroyed during his long stay in the Far East where he was thrown into constant contact with the British and made many warm personal friends among them. Whatever the reason may have been, he traveled far out of his way to get the service of a Paris tailor in preference to one in New York or London.

There was no doubt about the uniform being highly ornamental. It consisted of a blue single-breasted coat with standing collar lined with white silk, collar, cuffs and buttonholes embroidered in gold. The knee breeches of white twilled wool were ornamented with a stripe of gold braid, with gold knee buckles which matched the gold buckles on the shoes. Stockings were of white silk and the chapeau was ornamented with a black cockade and a gold eagle. A sword completed the regalia.

It is interesting to note that Secretary Marcy, who authorized this costume, shortly afterward got tired of the gaudy haberdashery worn by American diplomats and startled all of the chancelleries of Europe by a circular letter in which he suggested that, wherever practical, American diplomats "should wear the simple dress of the American citizen." A few years after his death, this suggestion was put into legal effect by Congressional action and gold braid, swords, and shoe buckles disappeared from the costumes of American diplomats.

Steamer connections on the Mediterranean-Suez route were complicated. Harris could have remained in Paris and by taking a steamer from Marseilles on December 4 would have reached Colombo in plenty of time to catch the steamer for Penang, but he "wished to avoid even the appearance of loitering," and so left Paris on November 26 although he knew that would mean an enforced wait of fifteen days in Colombo. As a matter of fact, he points out in his journal, he could have remained even longer in Paris and sailed on January 4 and still have been in plenty of time. Captain Bell of the *San Jacinto* had told him he did not expect to be in Penang before February 20. Captain Bell was optimistic. With constantly recurring engine trouble the American gunboat limped around the Cape and was more than a month late. Harris could not be blamed for wishing to linger on his first visit to Paris, for here was his last contact with the West and he knew that his exile would be a long one.

He arrived in Ceylon on Christmas Eve for a stay of a fortnight during which time he spent many hours in the small local library, the last he was to see for a number of years. During his stay he read: "The Newcombes" by Thackeray, "The Caxtons" by Bulwer-Lytton, "Alton Locke," "Yeast," "Hypatia" and "Westward Ho" by Kingsley, "Anti-Conigsby" by Disraeli, "Adventures in the Punjab" by Major Lawrence, "Charles I" by Guizet, "Life of Lord Metcalfe" by Kay. He found that Thackeray's realistic and somewhat cynical view of life left him with an unpleasant sensation. "In his eyes the whole world is base, black and faithless; he ignores everything like benevolent action based on principle, and disbelieves any other motive of action than egoism."

He was at once made pleasantly conscious of the dignities of his new office, for the local British officials called on him. When he had been in Colombo before as a mere private citizen he had called on them. The stiffness of the British colonial official melted in the presence of one who had the exalted rank of a Consul-General. If he had been accredited to a British port they would have fired salutes in his honor. On the day of his arrival he had dinner with the Acting Judge. Among the guests was a Presbyterian clergyman and Harris commented on the fact that he was a teetotaler "of which class the number is increasing in the East." Then he added reminiscently: "While in France I drank the delightful mild wine of the South, but after leaving Marseilles I came back to my old Asiatic habit—tea and cold water."

This was only the first of a series of entertainments. When he was in Ceylon before, he had been entertained only by his friends. Now even they were more cordial. "What a difference a title makes," he comments in his journal.

Harris accepted all this hospitality gratefully, for he was looking forward to his long exile in Japan where he knew he would have little opportunity to meet others of his own race and good dinners were problematical. Like most middle-aged bachelors he was appreciative of good food and well-served dinners, and his journal contains a good many detailed references to what he had to eat. With his residence in the East he had, like most other Americans, acquired exotic tastes including a fondness for curry; and like others found that a taste for good curry dooms one to almost constant disappointment when in Occidental countries. But Mrs. Forbes, the wife of a British official of Ceylon, served dinners and curries which aroused his enthusiastic praise. She entertained him at New Year's dinner

44

and while he found the company of the British army officers boring in the extreme, the food was superb.

The dinner was somewhat different from the usual English one in the colonies. A great number of excellent Cingalese *plates* made their appearance; among others, the cabbage, as it is called, of the cocoanut tree, dressed half a dozen different ways— the meat of the cocoanut which has just begun to germinate, in which state the cavity is quite filled up with a sweet, crisp, vegetable substance that is quite agreeable. The Malay curries of Mrs. Forbes were unexceptionable. *Hulway,* an Arab sweetmeat, made of rice, sugar and camel's milk, figured at the dessert among a regiment of Cingalese and Hindostanee preparations of fruit and sugars.

It was after this very satisfying dinner that he wrote in his journal: "This bids fair to be an important year for me. I have important matters entrusted to my charge and if I am successful, I may connect my name with the history of my country."

Then he continued: "But if unsuccessful, no matter what ability I may display in my negotiations I shall sink just as much in proportion as I should rise if successful. In other words, the world judges solely by results." ———

*Realistic*

## CHAPTER V

# THE LAND OF THE WHITE ELEPHANT

Aᶠᵗᵉʳ a belated arrival in Penang and a further delay while her engines were repaired, the *San Jacinto* finally anchored in the Gulf of Siam on April 13, 1856. It was not an inviting spot. The snake-infested waters of the Gulf were muddy and foul-smelling and there was no breeze from the sea to offer relief from the heat of the sun. Harris and his companions kept their eyes on a gap in the tree-lined shore which marked the mouth of the Menam, the crooked river which offered the only route to the pagoda-dotted capital of Bangkok. Everyone was anxious to get there as soon as possible for it was very hot and uncomfortable on the frigate.

Harris was more anxious than any of the others for he wanted to see this Siamese interlude over with so that he could get on to Japan and take up the more important duties that awaited him there. But the amenities of diplomacy had to be observed and before they could proceed any further toward Bangkok a letter had to be dispatched to the Minister of Foreign Affairs announcing their arrival.

Since Harris was accredited to two non-Christian countries, he had determined to show them an example of Christian behavior by refusing to transact any official business or hold any official interviews on Sunday. He had recorded this resolution in his journal, and in order to make sure he did not lose track of the days, he began

46

dating his journal with the day of the week as well as of the month. But in his first official act he violated this self-imposed pledge. In spite of the fact that the *San Jacinto* arrived off the mouth of the Menam on Sunday, he immediately wrote a letter to the Minister of Foreign Affairs. In this letter which announced his arrival he gave the names and the rank of all the officers of the ship and signed himself as: "Envoy Plenipotentiary of the United States of America to Siam and American Consul-General for the Empire of Japan."

His violation of the Sabbath had been justified in his eyes by the desire if not by the necessity for haste, but he was soon to learn that nothing could overcome the Siamese genius for delay and procrastination. During the ensuing daylight hours the Americans on the *San Jacinto* kept their eyes on the mouth of the Menam but it was not until the following Tuesday that a little blue steamer arrived bearing not only the flag of Siam but also the King's personal flag. The presence of the royal ensign led Harris to believe that this was an official call but the Prime Minister who soon came on board with his numerous suite insisted that he was incognito though he did not fail to bring with him all the insignia of his rank, including a large betel-nut box of solid gold and a solid gold teapot. He was accompanied by his sons, a few younger brothers, sword-bearer and servants. There was not room enough in the Siamese boat for all his younger brothers, numbering more than forty—the offspring of his father's numerous concubines.

The little steamer was the pride of Siam. It had been designed by a Siamese naval architect and built by native workmen, though the engine which broke down as frequently as the larger engines on the *San Jacinto* had been

47

brought from the United States. As it was the first steamer to be constructed in the country and for some time the only one, it was quite appropriately named *The Royal Siamese Steam Fleet,* a comprehensive title which the American visitors found irresistibly funny.

They were also vastly amused by the complicated etiquette of the country with its accentuated and absurd regard for rank and prestige. While the Prime Minister was walking about the deck, the stogie he was smoking went out and he called on a younger brother to light it for him. The American naval officers were both surprised and amused to see the young man throw himself on his knees and remain in that humble position until the stogie was satisfactorily lighted. Each nation marveled at the strange customs of the other. The red-stained mouths and blackened teeth of the betel-nut chewing Siamese aroused the disgust of the Americans whose accuracy in spitting out streams of tobacco juice was a matter of never ending interest to the natives. They were envious of the commodious spittoons on the ship.

Although the Prime Minister was visiting the ship incognito, he did not overlook an opportunity to do his bit for his country by attempts to delay the Americans' journey to Bangkok. As an interesting piece of gossip he passed out the information that the quarters provided for them were not so comfortable as those occupied by young Harry Parkes of the British mission, who had arrived a few days previously, and suggested that the Americans remain where they were until Parkes left, when they could move into the quarters he was now occupying. When Harris refused this suggestion he made another one, that before going to Bangkok Harris send two officers to inspect the quarters. But this idea also was declined. Harris was in a fever of impatience to start work after these months of inactivity. If the *San Jacinto* had not suffered so many breakdowns and had arrived on anything like schedule time he would have been in Bangkok long before the arrival of Parkes.

The Siamese had a particular reason for wanting to delay the proceedings, for they knew that a French mission was on its way to negotiate a treaty. They were in deadly fear that the British, French and Americans would join forces as Sir John Bowring had hinted they might do and so made every effort to keep representatives of the three nations separated. When Sir John had been in Bangkok a year before, they had endeavored to prevent his meeting the local American missionaries who constituted the entire foreign colony of the city. Their immediate object was to keep Harris and Parkes apart and to get the Englishman out of the way before they began the negotiation with the American. As Parkes had come to exchange the ratified copies of the treaty they did not anticipate that he would remain more than a few days.

Commissioner Harris and the officers of the *San Jacinto* assumed that the *Royal Siamese Steam Fleet* had come to take them to Bangkok and there was a hurried packing of personal effects, but the steamer went away without them and they resumed their tedious wait. It was not until Thursday, the fifth day after they had dropped anchor, that the steamer returned escorting the royal barges which were to convey them to the capital. The entourage which accompanied Commissioner Harris to Bangkok consisted of forty-two persons, including eight bandsmen whose instruments had been bought from the crew's "slush fund."

As Harris left the ship the *San Jacinto's* batteries fired a salute of seventeen guns. Dr. Wood, the fleet surgeon,

49

wrote that the salute was fired "to the President's letter, to the Consul-General, to the Commodore, or to all together" but Harris said the salute was for him. It was the first of many salutes to be fired in his honor and he never failed to note the number of guns and occasionally commented on the quantity of powder used in the charge. This question of the number of guns to be given in a salute was a very serious one then, as it is now, in naval and diplomatic circles, for while there are official regulations on the subject the commander of the gunboat can and often does use his own discretion in the matter. When Mr. Parkes had disembarked at Bangkok a few days previously, the British gunboat *Auckland* had given him a salute of eleven guns, although as a consul he was actually entitled to only nine, a fact which the officers of the *San Jacinto* were quick to note. Parkes called on Harris soon after the *San Jacinto* anchored and when he left, they followed the precedent which had been set by the *Auckland*. This was only one of many occasions when commanders of foreign gunboats in the Far East gave their own and other officials very liberal treatment in the matter of salutes as a means of impressing the natives. National rivalries and jealousies were forgotten in the presence of the Orientals and the two English-speaking nations were thrown into friendship by forces over which neither of them had any control.

Americans of that period were extremely sensitive about the growing power and prestige of their ancient enemy, Great Britain, which two successful wars with the country did not appear to have arrested. The professional jealousy which was shared by the naval officers may have been accentuated on the part of Commodore Armstrong of the *San Jacinto* as he had been captured and held a prisoner by the

50

British when a midshipman in 1814. But with a salute of seventeen guns to be fired a few days later for the American commissioner they could afford to be generous with the salute in honor of the British Consul.

A few hours after embarking from the *San Jacinto* the American party halted for refreshments at Nampok, half way to the capital, and one of the forty brothers of the Prime Minister who was acting as the official host impulsively suggested that a salute of twenty-one guns be fired in honor of the American flag which was being conveyed in one of the state barges. This was done at once, two American flags being borrowed from Harris for the purpose, one being hoisted on the fort and the other on the little blue steamer. With all their love of form and colorful ceremony it is perhaps significant that the Siamese had not provided themselves with a single American flag.

As they steamed up the bay towards Nampok, the ship's band which was crowded on the bow of the steamer struck up "Hail Columbia" which was tactfully changed to "God Save the Queen" as they passed under the stern of a British gunboat. There were a number of merchant ships in the harbor and the Americans were told that all of them were being loaded with rice for shipment to China by an adventurous American merchant who had just come to Bangkok from Shanghai. As the export of rice and salt had recently been prohibited, this was an illegitimate traffic, though carried on quite openly. But the illegitimacy was technical only, for prohibitions of this sort were not enacted by the government of Siam with any idea of enforcement but solely as a means of providing a new method of extorting bribes. The American merchant was a great personal friend of the first King and it was generally understood that the two were partners in this exportation of rice.

All along the crooked course of the Menam the banks were crowded with natives who had come out to see the American visitors. The band was the first they had ever heard and it provided a continuous show. The bandsmen played such American favorites as "Old Dog Tray" and "Old Folks At Home" and between these and other selections the bugles and drums were kept busy. At each stop presents of fruit were brought aboard, and the sailors who had been restricted to ship's fare for more than six months ate so much of it that many of them were sick the next day. One man had made his first acquaintance with fresh cocoanuts. The day was hot and he drank the milk from a hundred of them.

At the ceremonial pause for refreshments the Americans were not only delighted but greatly relieved by the cordial way in which they were met and the honors which were shown them. When the officers were escorted to the hall they noted that it consisted of platforms on three different levels and when Harris and the officers of the ship were given seats on the highest platform they knew that the first diplomatic victory had been won. Harris had been apprehensive and felt that the reception accorded them here would provide an index to what he might expect in Bangkok. The archives of the State Department contained reports on what had happened just six years before when Joseph Balestier had gone to Bangkok. On his arrival at Pagnam, he was told that the commanding officer was ill and the only officials who met him were those of low rank. At the official reception he was placed on the second platform of the hall, thereby indicating that he was a person of rank even lower than the minor Siamese officials who surrounded him. The most ignorant Chinese coolie who watched the proceedings from the outskirts of the crowd knew that an insult had been offered to the American envoy and to the flag which he represented, and Balestier was probably the only person present who did not know it. In a report to Daniel Webster, Secretary of State, he described the manner in which he had been received and said: "It was only after I returned to my barge that I was made aware of this rule of etiquette, and consequently of the affront put upon me. . . ."

This matter of rank as determined by the level at which one sat or stood was most important in the eyes of the Siamese who, like the Japanese, had borrowed their ideas of etiquette and ceremony from China. Sir John Bowring had been in Siam the year before and on one occasion when the Siamese officials called on him they found him waiting for them in a second-floor room just above the entrance. As the British diplomat had lived in China and was familiar with Oriental customs, there is some justification for the belief that he had arranged this deliberately. To reach this room the Siamese delegation would have to walk under it, thereby placing themselves for the moment in a position of inferior social rank, which was something they could not bring themselves to do. There was an awkward pause until a ladder was brought and placed against the side of the house, enabling the nobles to reach the upper room without passing under it.

Balestier's explanation that he did not know an affront had been offered to him was evidence of his unfitness for the task he had undertaken or for any diplomatic dealings with Orientals. It was remarkable that anyone, even with a brief residence in the Far East, or even one who was familiar with the significance of seating arrangements at a formal function of this sort would not have noted the intended slight. Balestier's ignorance was all the more remarkable considering the fact that he had served as Consul at Singapore for almost twenty years. However it is probable that his consular duties did not call for much more than the formalities of entering and clearing American ships and the occasional care of a distressed seaman.

When the Singapore Consul found that he had been made a laughing-stock he flew into a violent sea-captain's rage, quarreled with every Siamese official he came in contact with, and instead of a new treaty being negotiated, diplomatic relations between the two countries were worse than they were before. He said sharp words to the Siamese officials and they retaliated by sending a message to the American Government in which they said that the envoy was a "person of much excitability" and requested that if another envoy be sent "they may appoint an efficient prudent and well-disposed person, not inclined to anger." However the irascible envoy was not without his defenders. The local American missionaries apparently thought there were times when a wrathful tongue was justified, for they sent a letter to the State Department fully exonerating him.

About the time of this unpleasant episode Sir James Brooke, the English adventurer who had made himself Rajah of Sarawak, was sent to negotiate a new British treaty but was met with such hostile demonstrations that he also left without accomplishing anything. The Rajah was so disgusted with the treatment he had received, that as a gesture of contempt he gave his gold-braided court costume to "Old Gabriel," a half-breed Portuguese interpreter who was attached to the Siamese court. This gold braided costume, somewhat the worse for wear, aroused the curiosity of the Americans when they arrived.

Near the water's edge at Bangkok quarters for the American mission had been constructed—all of bamboo lashed together with fiber—not a nail or a piece of metal in the whole structure. The roof was made of dried palm leaves and though a tropical rain set in soon after the visitors' arrival, and continued for weeks, the rooms in the huge rambling structure remained perfectly dry. Wide strips of red and green silk had been used lavishly as decorations. One of the ship's officers commented on the fact that this structure must have cost the King of Siam a good deal more than the value of the presents brought to him. But in spite of their cost Harris found the quarters entirely inadequate. He had a bedroom all to himself but no room he could use for writing or for conferences. The bedroom had a doorway but no door and he used an American flag for a curtain. However he was much better off than Harry Parkes who had arrived with his bride only a few days before. They had found the large house put at their disposal swept clean but without a stick of furniture in it. They would have had no place to sleep if an American missionary had not invited the young couple to his home.

Theoretically the Americans were free to go and do as they liked. Actually they could not move from the doorstep without being accompanied by one or more of the guides and couriers who had been assigned to them and who, they felt sure, spied on them and reported their every movement to the court. Old Gabriel with his tattered British court costume was under foot all the time. He apparently thought it was one of the functions of visiting diplomats to supply him with appropriate costumes for he cast covetous eyes on the clothing of the naval officers, some of whom gave him garments they found uncomfortably heavy in this tropical climate. But, after their long confinement on board the ship, the Americans were all in a good humor and keen to enjoy the many new and unusual sights of this strange city.

The preliminary proceedings toward the negotiation for the treaty moved with more haste than was to be anticipated in an Oriental country, but the apparent haste proved later to be deceptive. The visitors were required to wait only two days before arrangements were made for Harris to pay his first official call on the Minister of Foreign Affairs. The visit was not a complete success, for Harris had yet to learn many things about the formalities of Oriental diplomacy. He made the call accompanied only by a few officers and the Minister was frankly disappointed that there was not a larger number. When Harris called on the Siamese nobles a few days later he was accompanied by the entire company of ship's officers and the band. There were more than forty people and it required four large boats to transport them.

In spite of the bad start the call on the Minister of Foreign Affairs was eminently satisfactory. After a few minutes of preliminary conversation during which each made perfunctory inquiries about the health of the other and the healths of their respective rulers, the subject of the treaty was brought up. Harris remarked that he presumed there would be no difficulty about it as the basis of the treaty he wanted to conclude was the one which Sir John Bowring had negotiated the previous year.

"We could yield no more than was granted in that

56

treaty," said the Minister. "The boat is already full, pressed to the water's edge and can bear no more."

The remainder of the interview was more encouraging. Through the American missionaries Harris had heard gossip to the effect that, as he did not represent a crowned head, he would not be given the same honorable treatment that had been accorded to Sir John Bowring as the representative of Queen Victoria; and that the letter of President Pierce would not be received personally by the King to whom it was addressed but by some subordinate official. Apparently this question had been discussed in official circles, for without waiting for the subject to be brought up the Minister explained to Harris that he would be received by the King in the same way that Sir John had been received and asked about a convenient time for the audience.

The British diplomat had been equally worried over fears that he would not be received with honors equal to those which had been accorded the envoy of Louis XIV who had visited Bangkok in 1683 in a vain attempt to add the King of Siam to the growing list of Catholic monarchs. The Siamese had tried to dodge this issue by saying they had no records of the formalities followed at this time but Sir John had prepared for this emergency by bringing a copy of the French envoy's diary in which everything had been set down with the most burdensome detail. This showed that the French officers had been allowed to wear their swords at the audience with the King, and Sir John successfully demanded the same privilege for the British mission.

Although he had been definitely promised that he would be given the same honors as had been accorded to Bowring, Harris still worried about it and was not satisfied until all

57

the details of the audience with the King had been arranged. The Siamese did not, in fact, keep their promise very punctiliously. Sir John had enjoyed several private conferences with the King before the formal public audience attended by all the nobles, and Harris asked for the same privilege but was refused. It was explained that the King had corresponded with Sir John for several years and he looked on him as an old friend and had received him privately in that capacity and not as the envoy of a foreign country. Harris was not satisfied with this explanation but he had to be content with it, for the King would not see him.

However, there was no fault to be found with the arrangements for the public audience, and the audience itself was as spectacular as anyone could wish. In the absence of any royal insignia Harris was determined to honor the letter of the President as Perry had done in Japan and, in fact, as Sir John had done with the letter of Queen Victoria. The arrangements made were that the letter was to be conveyed to the palace on a royal barge accompanied by the five standard-bearers with triangular silk banners and handed to the King by Harris himself without having to pass through the hands of an intermediary. In the audience chamber where the Siamese nobles would be compelled to sprawl humbly on the floor, velvet cushions were to be provided for Harris and Commodore Armstrong. The others were to sit on the carpet, but did not have to kneel or salaam like the Siamese nobles.

The letter itself was laid in a portfolio of embossed purple velvet; heavy white silk cords attached to the seal which was shut in a silver box ornamented in relief with the arms of the United States. The cords passing through the seal and box were terminated by two heavy white silk cord tassels; the whole was enclosed in a box in the form of a book bound in purple and gold; over this was thrown a cover of yellow satin.*

The yellow satin cover was an afterthought and had been bought by Harris when the *San Jacinto* anchored in Singapore. It was used to cover the list of presents which had been brought to the King.

The audience had been promised and postponed from time to time, then definitely sent for April 30, only to be postponed again by the King who could never resist the temptation to meddle and upset the arrangements made by his ministers. His reason for this postponement was that April was an unlucky month and he set May 1 as the date. This proved to be a lucky selection as far as the weather was concerned, for there was a pause in the rain which had fallen almost incessantly since the arrival of the Americans, and the day dawned bright and sunny. The first part of the trip, two miles up the Menam from the American quarters, was made in ceremonial state barges. At every dozen strokes the oarsman who acted as cox of the crew would let forth a loud yell and the other members of the crew would respond with low growls. The procession of boats extended for half a mile and the noise was terrific. When they arrived at the royal boat-landing there was more noise, for a salute of twenty-one guns was fired in honor of the President's letter. From the boat-landing to the palace it was necessary to be carried through the streets on chairs. The Americans were unused to this and looked so awkward and self-conscious that the Siamese crowd which lined the roadway could not restrain themselves and roared with laughter.

* *Fankwei* by William Maxwell Wood, M.D., U.S.N. Harper & Brothers, New York, 1859.

If Harris had been worried about the manner in which he and his party would be received, all doubts were set at rest from the time they left the boat-landing, for the whole show was produced and stage-managed in a way that any Hollywood producer might envy. Approaching the palace they passed through variegated files of infantry in which apparently every branch of the country's motley army was represented. A few of the soldiers were equipped with muskets and had uniforms of European style. Others wore long skirts of red calico and were armed with crossbows. With these effeminate costumes and antiquated weapons they wore military caps of modern design. The great variety of arms included pikes, battle-axes, spears and swords and poisoned arrows. There were "archers, single-headed spear companies, trident shaped spear companies, some with pikes, some with single swords, and other companies in which each man carried two swords; some carried oval shields and others only long narrow shields protecting only the arms." After passing this fantastic military display they came to another one even more striking. Twenty war elephants in full dress were lined up at the royal gates. On the back of each was mounted an ancient Spanish howitzer.

With each changing scene there were new displays designed to impress the visitors with the might and majesty of the Monarch of Siam. Inside the courtyard a hundred drums thundered a prelude to another salute of twenty-one guns. At the door of the audience hall the officials who had accompanied the Americans fell prostrate on the ground—and the lofty doors were thrown open to reveal a new spectacle which dazzled the visitors.

Along each side of the long hall, in two rows, lay the nobles of the kingdom, resting upon their elbows and knees upon red velvet cushions. They were clothed in the richest golden tissues, some heavy golden muslins over under-garments of rich silks, and some fine muslins over tunics of uniform gold.

Before each noble were ranged the ceremonial gold dishes, a betel-nut box, teapot and sword. The size of the teapot was presumed to indicate the rank of the owner, and some of them were as large as a soup tureen. One of the visitors estimated that there must have been between ten and twenty thousand dollars' worth of gold in front of each noble.

The audience continued for an hour and a half and the Americans were relieved to find that in spite of the sacredness of the King's presence and the strict formality of the proceedings, smoking and drinking were not prohibited—were in fact encouraged. Young nobles on their hands and knees pushed in front of the guests trays containing cigars and matches and decanters of wine. Harris and the Commodore and all the others smoked. The wine was not touched, probably owing to the recently formed temperance convictions of Commissioner Harris. Even when, at the dinner which followed, a toast and three cheers was proposed for the King of Siam, the Americans drank their toast "pro forma." One of the Siamese princes noted this and commented that they would cheer much more heartily if they would drink brandy as the British did.

At the end of the audience chamber was an elevated platform with a throne on which sat the King, even more gorgeously clad than his nobles, and wearing a purple velvet crown "glittering with jewels." In addition to the ceremonial guards with swords the King was protected by two other guards armed with business-like rifles. The throne was so high that Harris, who was not a tall man, had some

61

difficulty in handing the letter to the King. Having accomplished this he then delivered a short address, while the King impatiently fiddled with the box containing the President's letter and the list of presents like a child who is anxious to tear the wrappings off a new toy. The text of the address is reminiscent of the florid oratorical style of the period.

"The fame of Your Majesty's great acquirements in many languages and in the higher branches of science has crossed the great oceans that separate Siam from the United States, and has caused high admiration in the breast of the President." Then there followed a few words about America's fertile soil, manufacture and commerce. "The sails of its ships whiten every sea. Its flag is seen in every port. The gold mines of the country are among the richest in the world." After a suggestion that commerce between the two countries would be mutually beneficial Harris, in conclusion, referred to the King as "the wisest and most enlightened monarch of the East."

Harris probably believed that flattering reference was reasonably correct, for he had not yet met the King. As he became better acquainted with him he first called him a pedant, then a learned fool and finally came to the conclusion that he was weak minded. If King James was the most learned fool in Europe, the King of Siam was without doubt the most learned fool in the Orient.

## CHAPTER VI

## ADVENTURES IN DIPLOMACY

IT WAS not until after the glittering audience with the first King and another less spectacular audience with the second King that Harris had an opportunity to discuss his mission with the first King, who was in theory the absolute ruler of the country. There had been no formal negotiations regarding the treaty and the Siamese commissioners had not even been appointed, though there was no doubt in the mind of anyone that they would be the same as those who had negotiated the British Treaty. The King was reversing his former procedure. The formal audience with Sir John had been delayed until the treaty had been practically concluded, but with typical wilfulness the King now insisted that treaty negotiations could not begin until after the audience.

While waiting for the Siamese commissioners to be appointed Harris had plenty of time to learn something about the monarchs with whom he was dealing. The two Kings had not come to the twin thrones by an easy route. As the sons of their father's legal wife, they were due to succeed him, but on his death they had been displaced by an elder half-brother, the son of a concubine. As they were well aware of the dangers of being claimants to the throne, they timorously accepted this injustice without protest and sought only safety for themselves. The elder brother (now the first King) found refuge in a Buddhist monastery while the younger (the second King) set up a clock repair shop in Bangkok and had an English sign painted over the door of his workshop—

WATCHES AND CLOCKS REPAIRED HERE.

The period of seclusion lasted for more than twenty years and during this time the two brothers, although they prudently kept out of politics, rather ineptly prepared themselves for the possibility that some turn of fate might bring them to power. The encroachments of England on Burma and the Malay Peninsula as well as the growing French power in Cambodia and Cochin-China indicated to them, as it did to other observant Siamese, that their country could not much longer remain isolated and resist the influence of the West. There was, even at this time, what was known as a "Young Siam" party and the older brother prepared himself to be the leader of that faction. Though theoretically a recluse in a Buddhist monastery, he went to the Jesuit priests for instruction in foreign languages and modern science and they were only too happy to give him every assistance. The famous mission of Louis XIV to Siam had been sent by that pious monarch with the primary purpose of converting the King to Christianity, and though that venture had been a failure the Jesuits had continued their work; this opportunity to influence and possibly convert a prince who might some day rule the country fitted their evangelical plans.

With their assistance he learned a smattering of Latin and the natural sciences and astronomy, which he never completely disassociated from astrology, though he boasted of his ability to calculate eclipses. He also studied English. The American missionaries said they were his teachers but it appears more probable that he learned from the French priests. The queer dictionary brand of English which he spoke was rendered even more picturesque by the fact that he spoke with a French accent. He never got the proper salutations fixed in his mind and always startled foreign visitors by greeting them with "good-bye." As a letter writer he was probably the world's most industrious royal correspondent. He was so vain of his ability to write English that he wrote letters to people all over the world, and especially to scholars, for his smattering of Latin, French and English and astronomy had given him a delusion of scholarship which amounted to a mania. One of his early correspondents had been Sir John Bowring and this fact gave the British diplomat an entree to his friendship which probably could not have been gained by the mere fact that he was an envoy from Queen Victoria. The King was vastly impressed by the fact that Sir John had been given a degree by the University of Gronigen and was a member of such an imposing number of learned societies.

Although he never became a Christian, the teachings of the Jesuits and possibly of the American missionaries did give him a new concept of religion which might have had a profound effect on the civilization of Siam and on Buddhism itself if he had been a man of ability and strong character. When he became First King he ordered expunged from the sacred books of that religion all reference to the complicated cosmogony, retaining only its moral precepts, with the idea that the teachings of Buddhism would not be an obstacle to the acceptance of Western science. He went even farther and made one attempt definitely to link science with Buddhism. In one of the temples in Bangkok which he maintained there appeared above the orthodox

Buddhist pictures a correct representation of the solar system. His position in the Buddhist world was unique. Since the two other ancient strongholds of Buddhism, India and Ceylon, had come under British rule, Siam was the only independent country with a Buddhist King, and he was looked upon as the political head of the church. Although his revised version of Buddhism was not accepted by the fundamentalists in the Buddhist monasteries, it did constitute what might be called a pure religion in that articles of faith were not confused with complicated Oriental theories as to how and why the world was created. But like many other Oriental reforms this one existed in theory only.

The younger of the two brothers remained in Bangkok in the political obscurity of his watch repair shop and was the pupil of the American missionaries. He spoke and wrote English with more ability than the elder brother but was less pedantic and had a fair amount of common sense.* His tastes were practical rather than academic and his watch repair trade had given him some mechanical skill for he constructed a steam engine in all its parts with his own hands. His library was full of English books and he was foolishly proud of his foreign knowledge. He had even given his oldest son a foreign name and Sir John Bowring was gratified to learn that in the Siamese nobility there was a

* The second King wrote Sir John Bowring a letter which he assumed was in the King's own handwriting as the signature was written in the same hand as the text. A year later he wrote a similar letter to Harris. Both diplomats commented on the beauty of the penmanship and preserved the letters which were later reproduced in facsimile in the book about Siam written by Bowring and in the published journal of Townsend Harris. A casual examination of the letters shows that they were written by different persons, probably by two clerks. Neither of the two diplomats appeared to know that in the Orient a signature means nothing and that the authenticity of a document is attested to by a seal.

66

young man with the typically British name of Prince George. When Americans arrived, they learned that the complete name was George Washington. Sir John didn't know that. While the older brother took a childish pride in exhibiting his pedantic accomplishments, the younger was equally infantile in his pride over his scientific learning and his ability to use foreign tools.

When the usurper died the two brothers were called from the monastery and the clock repair shop to occupy their respective thrones. Each had come to power at maturity and neither had the training or the background for a royal position. The King was crowned on April 2, 1851. Some American waggishly suggested that it would have been highly appropriate to have crowned him one day earlier, on April Fool's Day. It is significant of the tangled intrigues of the country that they were not made Kings because they were the rightful claimants to the thrones but because one of their partisans controlled enough military strength to browbeat the other nobles.

This partisan, who was rewarded with the post of Prime Minister, was believed by many to be an honest patriotic reformer who thought that by bringing the older brother from his monastery he would establish the "Young Siam" party in power and bring about reforms including the establishment of better conditions for the overtaxed and servile people. If these were his plans they proved vain. Before he came to the throne the Prince and the Prime Minister had been the best of friends but after he came to power the King forgot his liberal ideas and political gossip said he was jealous of the Prime Minister's influence and abilities. As soon as he was released from his monastic vows, the newly created King devoted his attention to the establishment of a harem which soon included no less than 700 concubines who had more than 2,000 female attendants. He divided his time between the harem and letter writing and used his great authority in childish, petty ways. Harris said that the King resembled Solomon only in respect to the number of wives and concubines he maintained. His letters were full of pedantic nonsense but neither in them nor in the many conferences he had with Sir John Bowring and Townsend Harris did he discuss any of the problems of government. It appears that he was not even familiar with any of the copy-book maxims of other rulers or he would have shown off his learning by quoting them. The second King, who occupied a powerless ornamental position similar to that held by the Vice-President of the United States, did not tempt fate by playing any part in politics.

The flair for a pretension to scholarship seems to have been a family trait for a third brother who had managed to pick up some knowledge of Western medicine, probably from the American missionaries, had set himself up as a doctor and on the rise of the family fortunes became the Royal Physician. His complaints to the surgeon of the *San Jacinto* about being overworked were doubtless justified. The care of the King's harem alone provided him with more patients than would be cared for by the average family practitioner. He had one diploma from some medical school in Philadelphia and a second one showing that he was a member of the New York Academy of Medicine. In addition to his duties as Royal Physician he also helped in treaty negotiations and was one of the first court officials with whom the Americans came in contact.

At his first interview with the Prime Minister Harris found that his loyalty to the monarchial idea appeared to be tinged with a certain amount of skepticism. There was no permanency about their government, he said. They had no legislative body.

The accidental disposition and intelligence of the Monarch controlled everything and kings in a few generations forgot that they sprang from the people, and lost all sympathy with them. It was essential to the prosperity of a nation that it should have fixed laws, and that nobles should be restrained from oppressing the people, otherwise the latter were like chickens who, instead of being kept for their eggs, were killed off.*

The Americans wondered whether these words represented his own sentiments or merely something he had read in a book and repeated for effect. He had expressed similar sentiments in almost the same phraseology to Sir John who was equally skeptical as to their sincerity. As both the American and the British plenipotentiaries hurried away from Siam as soon as the treaties were concluded, neither of them left any record as to their final conclusions; but there was no evidence that the Prime Minister ever sacrificed any of his own great wealth and power for the benefit of the people.

It was supposed that the audiences with the two Kings would clear the way for the active negotiation of the treaty, but there was delay after delay. On May 5 Harris had been in the country for twenty-two days and the commissioners had not yet been appointed. The Siamese advanced many reasons for this delay, some plausible and some only silly. At one time a day had been set for meeting the commissioners when matters were further delayed because the King had suddenly decided to draw up all papers in English. The real reason for the series of delays was that the brilliant

* Fankwei by William Maxwell Wood, M.D., U.S.N.

young British diplomat, Harry Parkes, had brought the ratified copy of the Bowring Treaty back from London and was still in Bangkok trying to come to an agreement as to the interpretation of some of its terms. The Siamese were anxious to get this problem settled and Parkes out of Siam before they took up the matter of the American treaty, for they were afraid of joint action by the two countries.

The two visiting diplomats presented a strange contrast. Harris, who was in his fifty-second year, was enjoying his first diplomatic experience, while Parkes at twenty-eight was a veteran in the British diplomatic service. At the age of fourteen he had been employed in the translator's office of the mission of Sir Henry Pottinger to China and had been present at the signing of the Treaty of Nanking. Later he had served as Consul at Amoy and had accompanied Bowring to Siam as his secretary. Though the latter gave him but little credit for his work there is good reason to believe that it was due to his efforts, rather than those of his chief, that the treaty had been so successfully concluded.

In the meantime there was a continual round of official and private parties and visits and Harris had to endure the horrors of Siamese cooking with the "meat almost raw and everything surcharged with onions, garlic and leeks." There was an occasional welcome respite from Siamese cooking when meals in Chinese style were served. Harris usually ate too heartily on these occasions and soon his chronic gastric troubles were complicated by an eruption of boils. The combination of indigestion, boils and the fickleness and unreasonableness of the officials tried his patience as it had never been tried before. Every official visit was a musical affair, for the Americans trailed their band about with them wherever they went. The Siamese liked it and one suspects that one reason why so many invitations were pressed on the visitors was that they could be depended upon to put on a good show. In fact most of the invitations embodied a request that the band be brought along. It was diplomacy set to music and relieved the Americans of many half-hours of tedious conversation and probably accomplished a more useful purpose. The King always insisted on the presence of the band and all doubts as to his childish mentality were set at rest when he had his own orchestra and the band play different selections at the same time.

Knowing the frugality with which the American government dispensed diplomatic gifts, Harris discouraged any discussion of them, but that did not prevent the Siamese bringing up the subject. The fat, good natured Royal Physician cadged surgical instruments from the surgeon of the *San Jacinto* and almost everyone with whom the Americans came in contact wanted something. Soon the two Kings had all the gifts and there was nothing for the nobles. The State Department had not trusted Harris to distribute the gifts to the best advantage, but had carefully allocated every item, leaving many as disappointed as children who have been overlooked at Christmas. An official whose duties corresponded with those of a royal treasurer had no compunction about asking Harris to send him a present of a sword from Japan and went into details as to the kind he wanted, its length and how it should be decorated. He was modest in his request to Harris, for he had asked Bowring for two swords. He probably thought the value of the gift should be adjusted to the wealth of the two countries. He was shocked to learn what a small salary the President received— only $25,000 a year—and was frankly skeptical when assured that he had no private graft of any sort.

The Americans were very lucky in the matter of the gifts brought on the *San Jacinto*. Sir John had been liberal in his promises and Parkes had left London loaded up like a royal Santa Claus, but when the British gifts were being transferred from one ship to another at Singapore a careless boatman allowed the cargo to slip into the bay and only a few of the many presents were salvaged. The American gifts all arrived in good condition. For fear the concussions might shatter the large ornate mirrors, Commodore Armstrong violated navy regulations by dispensing with the usual monthly target practice, though he did go through the pretense of firing at targets with blank charges.

The King finally drew up the powers of the commissioners in a form to his own satisfaction and the first meeting was held. Secretary Marcy had given Harris instructions as to what form the treaty should take but in the negotiations at Bangkok the copy of the English treaty was used as the model. Perhaps this treaty embodied all that Marcy contemplated and Americans may possibly have helped in drafting the original proposals put forward by the British. In his journal Bowring says: "It was the intention of Mr. McLane, the American Commissioner, to proceed with me to Siam, but the state of his health and the necessity of visiting Europe led to the abandonment of his purpose." If this is true, and there is no reason to doubt it, the two countries must have come to an understanding as to what the treaty should contain. However, there was no suggestion of co-operation in Secretary Marcy's letter of instruction. On the other hand there were instructions that advantage be taken of any resentment or suspicion which the growth of England's power in the Far East may have aroused in the minds of the Siamese. Marcy wrote:

It is obvious that you will be at no loss for an argument to show the difference between the foreign policies especially of this country and Great Britain. While the latter is herself an Eastern power and as such by the late Burmese War has become a near neighbor to Siam, we covet no dominion in that quarter. It is undoubtedly to the interest of Siam to be liberal in her commercial policy towards the United States.

At the time Secretary Marcy was disclaiming any desire for expansion in the Far East he was carrying on a very active intrigue to secure the annexation of Cuba.

Harris, however, was not satisfied that he would do his complete duty by accepting the British Treaty as it was; he had in mind a few amendments. The most important was a concession to Americans to work the tin and other mines on a royalty basis. One by one all of the amendments he proposed were rejected and when after days of argument he wearily agreed to accept the British Treaty as it stood, a new hitch came over the question of the right of Americans to purchase land in Bangkok. The British Treaty provided that British subjects would have this right after a residence of ten years, the theory being that the ten year period would give them time to learn the language and become familiar with the customs of the country. As there were at the time the treaty was drawn no British subjects living in the country, the Siamese had agreed to this provision readily, for the problems and difficulties it presented would not have to be solved for a decade.

But the theory by which these rights had been postponed so far as the British were concerned would not apply to the American missionaries, as all of them had lived in Siam more than ten years and had nothing more to learn about the country. The situation was further complicated by an un-

fortunate incident. One of the missionaries had evaded the
law by the purchase of some property in the name of his one
female convert, who was also a servant in his household.
She was imprisoned and brought to trial and, although ac-
quitted, the affair left a bad impression in the minds of the
Siamese.

The British Treaty also provided for the mutual protection
of British subjects in Siam and of Siamese subjects in British
territory. The Prime Minister at once objected that a provision of this sort meant something in the British Treaty as
there were many Siamese subjects in neighboring British
territory but there were none in the United States. He added
that if any of his countrymen ever took up a residence in a
land so distant they would be considered as having left
Siam for good. One of the officers of the *San Jacinto* had
told the Prime Minister a few days previously that the
Siamese twins were living in America but apparently there
were no other Siamese in the country. He suggested as an
equivalent that American gunboats protect Siamese shipping
from pirates and that American Consuls in all parts of the
world extend their protection to distressed Siamese.

Harris would have omitted the British provision that
opium could be imported duty free but the Siamese per-
versely insisted that this be included. When Roberts negotiated his treaty he had attempted to legitimatize the importation of opium but had failed because of the stubborn
opposition of the Siamese.

The Siamese refused to agree to any clauses which were
not included in the British Treaty and then with exasperating Oriental logic tried to get Harris to accept less than
had been granted to the other country. In a long and flowery
preamble the Prime Minister declared his people's love for

74

Americans because they were not seeking conquests in the Far East and because of the helpfulness of American missionaries. The English, on the other hand, were a rapacious race bent on seeking all of Asia for themselves. The treaty which they had concluded with Sir John Bowring had not been made because of their love for the English but because they feared them.

"Now," said the Prime Minister with the appearance of driving home a point which none could dispute, "you who are our friends and whom we esteem, surely you will not ask as much from us as we were forced to give to our enemies?"

There was a great deal more talk along the same line. In a letter to the State Department Harris reported:

In my confidential interviews with the ministers, they expressed both fear and hatred of England. They read in the history of Burmah the fate that probably awaits them, and which they consider only a question of time. They were most anxious to be taken under the protection of the United States. They plainly told me that if I would make a treaty of alliance, they would give us all we could ask, even to a monopoly of trade.

Harris gave evasive replies to these proposals. He knew that a treaty of alliance was absurd, that a monopoly of trade could not be enforced. The Siamese also knew it, for when Harris tried to get a concession for Americans to work the tin mines, the Siamese promptly pointed out that any concessions given to the Americans would also have to be given to the British and the French. It was mere idle talk which did nothing but prove the fears in which the Siamese held the British, fears which Harris had obviously not discouraged.

After the main part of the treaty had been decided on (practically a copy of the British Treaty) and there were no more important differences to be discussed, the Prime Minister produced a new preamble written by the King himself which would have made the document absurdly topheavy. It was a complete and detailed history of the diplomacy of the country over a period of thirty years, giving the names and titles of all the envoys sent to Siam and a lot of details which were not even of local historical importance. Harris insisted that it did not comport with the dignity of the United States to have the names of third parties inserted in a simple commercial treaty and although the Prime Minister did not express any agreement with him, he dropped the matter, only to present a few days later another troublesome suggestion.

This was that the preamble which had been used in the Roberts Treaty also be used in this one. There was nothing objectionable to the Roberts preamble except that the language was florid, even for that period. The King was referred to as "His Majesty the Sovereign and Magnificent King" and the hope was expressed that the commercial intercourse established by the treaty would continue "as long as heaven and earth endure." Such language as this was calculated to be irritating to any honest man. To refer to the dawdling, quibbling pedantic monarch as a "Magnificent King" was a travesty and the principal reason a new treaty was needed was that for all practical purposes the Roberts Treaty had endured only until the nobles could devise a means of circumventing its provisions. Harris, whose nerves were on edge because of illness and the long delays, took a malicious dig at the King by objecting that the preamble was not in good English, was ungrammatical and would be laughed at.* This was not correct but it did silence the King

* See Cosenza's, *The Complete Journal of Townsend Harris*, page 152.

for a time though he brought it up again just as the text of the treaty was being engrossed. The King had some grounds for insisting on the flattering reference to himself for the letter from President Pierce had been addressed:

"To His Majesty, The Magnificent King of Siam."

Harris had just made a written reply to this final request when a new one was brought up, that in one of the three copies of the treaty, the Kings of Siam would be named first. Thanks to their experience with the Bowring Treaty they offered no objections to signing more than one copy. When the Roberts Treaty was negotiated the suspicious officials had refused to sign a duplicate copy of the document for fear Roberts would sell it to some third power.

But all things have to come to an end, even diplomacy in Siam, and the treaty was signed on May 29, 1856. There were thirty-six signatures and seals to be attached to each of the three copies of the treaty and it was three hours before the task was completed.

Suffering from boils and indigestion, his apparently untiring patience exhausted by the long-drawn-out proceedings, Harris wrote in his journal:

My mind is greatly relieved and I hope this is the end of my troubles with this false, base and cowardly people. To lie here is the rule from the Kings downward. Truth is never used when they can avoid it. A native or slave, each must crawl prone on his belly in the presence of some superior, and in turn he strives to increase the number of *his* prostrate inferiors. This custom causes them to seek the company of those inferior to themselves. I have never met a people like them, and I hope I may never again be sent here. The proper way to negotiate with the Siamese is to send two or three men-of-war of not more than sixteen foot draft of water. Let them arrive in October and at once proceed up to Bangkok and fire their salutes. In such case the treaty would not require more days than I have consumed weeks.

In a longwinded letter which the King wrote to accompany the treaty he said:

We have perused and seen and understood the whole contents of this Treaty, and found both English and Siamese very nearly similar a copy of the Treaty made with the English plenipotentiaries, only such changes in names of persons and country and of form as would be proper in a treaty between Siam and America, etc., etc.

The letter was written in his usual verbose style, one sentence containing more than 300 words. He signed himself as "The First King of Siam and Dependencies, reigning 2223 days ago." Other sovereigns might calculate dates by the year of their reign but he calculated them by days.

After all of the unnecessary delays, Harris had to endure a final one which was even more unnecessary and exasperating than the others. The King had asked him to postpone his departure from Saturday morning to the afternoon so that he could be received in a final audience. Harris, who could not refuse the request, was up at 5 o'clock so as to have plenty of time, but the boats which were supposed to call for him at seven o'clock did not arrive until after eight. When he and his party arrived at the palace they were kept waiting for nearly two hours before the King received them. At the audience the King driveled on for hours about his many scholastic accomplishments and when he could think of nothing more to say, insisted that Harris and his party wait until he wrote a longwinded letter to Sir John Bowring for Harris to deliver in Hongkong.

On the ratification of the treaty the famous American firm of Russell & Co. established offices in Bangkok and other American merchants moved in to take advantage of the new opportunities for trade. British and French concerns also came about the same time, but none of them prospered to the extent that they had anticipated. Russell & Co. moved out after a few unprofitable years and the other American firms soon followed. With their traditional policy of making the State Department pay its own way, Congress refused to appropriate any salary for the Consul and allowed him only to keep the fees which he collected. At first these fees provided a satisfactory income but as the American merchants moved away and there was less and less American shipping the fees finally dwindled to a point where they were not sufficient to pay the expense of the boat the Consul needed for his official duties. Local missionaries kept the consular flag flying as a patriotic duty but in the end the unrewarded work became too onerous and no one could be found to fill the post.

Even with their dull sense of humor the Siamese must have found it funny that a wealthy nation like the United States would go to so much trouble to secure the right to appoint a Consul to their country and then balk at the expense of maintaining one. Harris received no acknowledgment from the State Department of the work that he had done until more than two years later when he was informed that printed copies of the treaty would be sent to him.

## CHAPTER VII

## THE TEDIOUS ROAD TO JAPAN

AFTER all the delay in Bangkok, Harris and the small official party which had remained with him in the capital went on board the little blue steamer *The Royal Siamese Steam Fleet* on Saturday afternoon, May 31, glad to know that they were no longer treading the soil of Siam, and that they would soon be out of the garbage-infested river. They were even tired of the pagodas, the curious peaked roofs and the frangipanni trees and the picturesque costumes of the people, which they had found so interesting only a short time before. They had been glad to get away from the restricted quarters of the *San Jacinto* but after the deceit, chicanery and artificially conventional life of Siam, the frigate flying the American flag appeared an oasis of liberty, and in their new perspective her decks were remembered as being uncramped and spacious. They were looking forward to a good supper and hoped there would be baked beans and big navy mugs of hot coffee.

All the American residents of Bangkok were down at the river edge to see them off and gave them three hearty cheers. The band, which had remained with the official party to the last, played "Hail Columbia," "The Star-Spangled Banner" and "Yankee Doodle." Harris shared the hopes of the others that there would be a good supper on the *San Jacinto* for all were heartily tired of Siamese cooks with their predilection for leeks and garlic and the hurried manner in which they roasted meats. Harris, the oldest man in the party, had suffered the most. At the very first meal he ate in Siam he had regretfully recorded the fact that while the fruit was abundant and delicious, the meats were cooked atrociously. Politeness as well as his very hearty appetite had compelled him to eat food which he did not like and as a result his stay in Siam had been punctuated by constantly recurring attacks of indigestion and he was still suffering from boils.

The brave little steamer was barely out of sight of the landing when there was a halt of a half-hour to fix the machinery. The engines turned noisily for a half-hour longer and then there was another halt. With these delays the short tropical twilight was on them when they approached Paknam and as the crooked channel of the river was unlighted it was apparent that they could travel no farther and would have to throw themselves on the hospitality of the Governor and spend the night there. This was an unexpected visit and the usual tedious Siamese etiquette was forgotten while the governor hustled around and brought out tea, coffee, cakes and fruit. At eleven o'clock he managed to serve a hot meal to all of those who had not in the meantime gone to sleep. At five in the morning Harris, the early riser, had them all up and after some tea, coffee and fruit they were off again to the hospitable *San Jacinto*. A thunder-storm broke out after they got into the gulf and rain fell so thick that the shore could not be seen. The second King, who had supervised the building of *The Royal Siamese Steam Fleet*, had forgotten to put a compass aboard her and there was nothing to do but to drop anchor and wait until the rain ceased and a landfall could be seen. Finally the sun came out and they were happy to see the good old *San Jacinto* only a short distance away.

Engine trouble appeared to be contagious, for they had steamed only a few miles when something went wrong with the *San Jacinto's* engines—something so seriously wrong that it could not be repaired at sea and they limped along toward Hongkong at less than five miles an hour. They had started precisely at noon on Sunday and they traveled with the speed of a plowhorse all that afternoon, Monday, Tuesday, Wednesday, Thursday, Friday, and Saturday. Then in a dead calm the ship was stopped and another attempt made to repair the engines so as to avoid the humiliation of hobbling into the British port in a crippled condition. The weather was hot and there was no breeze and everyone was thoroughly miserable and uncomfortable. The only cheerful note recorded in Harris' journal was the fact that he had been able to help the naval officers in navigation, for they were unfamiliar with this part of the world. He had been through the South China Sea a number of times. On the following Thursday they were able to anchor off Hongkong —eleven days for a voyage of less than 2000 miles. Harris had just missed one of the infrequent mails by which he had hoped to advise President Pierce of the success of the Siam negotiations.

There were a few busy days in Hongkong with many letters to write and long reports to Secretary Marcy about the business in Siam. One of the first personal letters Harris wrote was to Commodore Perry who had at one time hoped to make a treaty with Siam and was one of the many distinguished correspondents of the letter-writing King. Harris and Sir John Bowring, now the Governor of Hongkong, exchanged reminiscences about their experiences in Siam and Peter Parker, the missionary-doctor who was acting as American Commissioner to China, called. Harris and Sir

John had been friends in Hongkong when Harris lived there and their experiences in Siam gave them a new common interest. The British official had hoped to be sent to Japan to make a treaty for his country, and if the seriousness of the situation in China had not made it necessary for him to remain in Hongkong he would probably have preceded Harris in Japan as he had in Siam. But as the honor of making, or attempting to make, the first treaty was going to Harris, the British diplomat gave him all the help possible. No matter which country made the treaty the other would benefit by it, just as America had benefited by the British Treaty in Siam. Sir John, thinking of the benefits to be gained by his country, rather than of his own personal prestige, heartily wished Harris every success, gave him friendly and helpful advice and supplied him with copies of diplomatic papers which were not available in the State Department at Washington. Included in them was complete information as to the Dutch trade monopoly at Nagasaki. During the time that Harris was in Japan the two exchanged frequent letters and the British diplomat continued to give Harris a great deal of assistance. During this period the British and American governments were at loggerheads and there was frequent talk of war, but in the Far East the representatives of the powers were on friendly terms and worked together on their local problems. In one of his first dispatches to Secretary Marcy, Harris said that as soon as one got east of Suez, the talk of war between America and England began to diminish.

Dr. Peter Parker, who was one of the first to call on Harris, was very unpopular with the Americans living on the China Coast. He was regarded as a fussy old trouble-maker and a great many had hoped that Harris would be appointed in his place. He was full of suggestions as to how Harris should comport himself for he was proud and vain of his slender Japanese experience. In 1837 Parker had been one of a group of young American missionaries living in Macao and Canton who had made an unofficial attempt to establish relationships with Japan by returning a group of Japanese shipwrecked sailors. They had borrowed an idle American sailing-ship for the purpose but their mission failed completely. They had not only not been allowed to land, but had been compelled to take the sailors back to Macao. The only thing gained by the enterprise was the fact that S. Wells Williams, one of the missionary adventurers, had learned something of the Japanese language from the shipwrecked sailors which was to be of great help to him when he served as interpreter on the Perry expedition. Although a missionary, Parker was the most militant of the diplomats—so militant in fact that his French and British colleagues could not follow him.

In Hongkong Harris made the final preparations for his long exile in Japan, arranged for additional food supplies and employed a cook and his helper, a tailor, a washman, and a butler or head boy. The cook had pretended to be an expert in the matter of curries and Harris arranged for an additional supply of curry powder and chutney to be sent from Calcutta.

The defective engines of the *San Jacinto* had not been repaired at sea and an examination at Hongkong showed the trouble to be very serious. Repair work started as soon as they anchored but after more than a week of work Commodore Armstrong reported that it would be another twelve to fifteen days before they would be ready to start for Japan. The frigate had been delayed from the beginning

84

of the voyage by trouble with the engines. At one time before rounding the Cape the fires had been drawn and she got along as best she could under her own sail. She had arrived in Penang in a crippled state and there had been another delay for repairs.

On July 4 Harris was still in Hongkong, daily growing more exasperated. The American Consul-General gave a large dinner party in honor of the day but Harris did not attend because of a "wish to avoid all such affairs which are sure to run into excess of noise and drinking." It turned out to be a gay party which would not have suited his tastes, for it didn't break up until two in the morning.

He finally said farewell to all of his friends and went on board the *San Jacinto* early on the morning of July 9 expecting the frigate to be ready to sail before noon but found the engineers still pottering around with repairs. They continued to work all that day and all night and the frigate finally got away at dawn. The journal does not state whether or not any salutes were fired or other formalities observed. Probably not. If guns were fired, the next few minutes provided a ridiculous anti-climax. The frigate had proceeded only one mile when there was a series of terrific blows and the whole ship was shaken before the engine could be stopped. An examination showed that the propeller shaft had come loose and the blades were tearing at the outer stern posts.

This was not a repair job the engineers could undertake. Indeed the long series of mishaps the ship had suffered would appear to indicate that they were not competent to keep the vessel in repair. This time they did not try to patch things up themselves but sent for help, and two days later the frigate was ignominiously towed by a couple of merchantmen to the dock at Whampoa for repairs. In order to lighten the vessel so that she could enter the dock all the stores of coal had to be removed as well as the guns. A man-of-war traveling under such humiliating conditions is supposed to be incognito and is not required to give or answer salutes, but as she went by the British frigate *Nankin*, the British band struck up a hearty "Hail Columbia." The Americans did not know whether it was a compliment or a taunt.

"A trying day for me," Harris confided to his journal. "I am losing some fourteen dollars a day salary besides the wages of my servants, some sixty dollars a month."

The State Department had provided that his salary of $5,000 a year would not begin until he arrived at his post of duty. He had now been serving the department for almost a year, his pay had not yet begun and he was still more than a thousand miles from his post. He wrote impatiently to Secretary Marcy telling him of this last mishap to the *San Jacinto*, adding that he would not be delayed further but would proceed at once to Japan by the first available steamer. Fortunately he did not have an opportunity to carry out this rash threat as there were no steamers going to Japan. He later had trouble enough with the Japanese officials when he arrived accompanied by a gunboat. If he had arrived in an ordinary merchant steamer there would have been almost unsurmountable obstacles.

He had paid his formal farewell calls at Hongkong and rather than be embarrassed by returning he went to the nearby Portuguese colony of Macao where Captain Drinker maintained a summer home. There he idled away the time until August 8 when he got up at daybreak to go to Hongkong to join the *San Jacinto* for the second time only to find that he would still have to wait a few more days.

It had rained all the time he was in Macao and he complained about the lack of exercise. It was still raining in Hongkong when he arrived there and he got his exercise in ship-board style by walking five miles a day on the veranda. Among the few letters he received was one from an old friend who assured him that Buchanan was sure to be elected President and that under a Democratic administration he could stay in Japan as long as he liked.

The Chinese servants he employed had been given an advance of three months' wages and while idling away their time in Macao the temptations of the *fan tan* table had been too strong for them. The tailor came to him with a sad tale of having lost all of his money and asked an advance of five dollars which Harris refused. Later, the Chinese butler told him the whole story. The tailor had not only lost all his money but in an unsuccessful attempt to recoup his fortunes had pawned his clothing and his sleeping mat and needed the five dollars to redeem them. Harris again refused the money but redeemed the articles himself and took them on board the *San Jacinto*.

The tailor absconded soon after they reached Hongkong and when he could not be found Harris demanded that his guarantor make good the $42 advanced as wages. In twenty minutes after this demand was made the tailor, bound hand and foot, was brought to him by the guarantor. He was sent on board the *San Jacinto* with instructions by Harris that he be held as a prisoner. He escaped again the next day and the bondsman had to hunt him up a second time.

After a few tedious days in Hongkong the repairs on the frigate were again said to be completed, the coal and the

87

guns put on board and everyone was ready to sail—everyone but the purser; there was a delay of another day until he got his papers in order. Finally they got away on August 12 in a rain storm. But the weather was fine next day. The engines were working smoothly; there was no trouble with the propellers. All sails were set and the ship clipped along at eight miles an hour. Later, as the breeze stiffened this was increased to more than eleven miles.

As they left the shelter of the Pescadores and proceeded north by east toward Formosa it began to appear that the delay at Hongkong may have been a fortunate one, for a typhoon had swept the China Coast and they ran into a number of dismasted and otherwise disabled junks. With the propellers out of commission, a violent typhoon would have been very dangerous.

Some time was lost in helping the disabled junks, and then on August 16 something again went wrong with the machinery. Water had collected in the air pumps and the packing in the stuffing boxes had blown out. This had been one of the causes of delay as they were leaving Siam. Harris observed that he "could not help thinking that these accidents to our machinery arise in some degree from carelessness among the engineers." It appeared that during the idle month they had spent in Siam it had not occurred to any one of the twelve engineers to make an inspection and see that everything was in order. Quite obviously discipline on board the *San Jacinto* had been relaxed—perhaps the officers resented the task of providing transport to a civilian. When Roberts had gone on his mission to Siam the officers of the frigate on which he traveled refused to provide quarters for him and he had been compelled to sleep on deck with the gun crew.

Irascible Mr. Balestier had also been very shabbily treated by the navy. The Siamese humiliated him, but in doing so they only followed the precedent set by the American naval officers who did not give him the ceremonial support he had a right to expect and did not accompany him to Paknam. The fact that he arrived there practically alone was in itself a slight to the Siamese authorities. He was not the first nor the last American diplomat to experience the contempt in which the American naval officer of that period held all civilians. Harris appeared to get along very well with Commodore Armstrong and was personally very popular with the junior officers but he was later to feel the brunt of departmental jealousy and be shamefully neglected.

The defective air pumps were finally patched up and the *San Jacinto* entered Japanese water. On sight of the first outlying Japanese island Harris wrote hurriedly and sketchily, like one whose thoughts were traveling very much faster than his pen could record them:

Conflicting emotions are caused by the sight of these Japanese possessions. My future brought vividly to mind. Mental and social isolation on the one hand, and on the other are important public duties which, if properly discharged, will redound to my credit. A people almost unknown to the world to be examined and reported on in its social, moral and political state; the productions of the country to be ascertained; the commercial intercourse, what are its wants, and what it has to give in exchange. A new and difficult language to be learned; a history, which may throw some light on that of China and Korea, to be examined; and finally the various religious creeds of Japan are to be looked at. These various matters offer abundant occupation for my mind, and will surely prevent anything like ennui being felt if I only give myself heartily to the work, and if that *sine qua non* of all earthly possessions—health—be vouchsafed to me by the Great Giver of all good.

After recording these reflections in his journal he could not sleep so greatly was he oppressed by a sense of his responsibilities. The following day he wrote:

I shall be the first recognized agent from a civilized power to reside in Japan. This forms an epoch in my life and may be the beginning of a new order of things in Japan. I hope I may so conduct myself that I may have honorable mention in the histories which may be written on Japan and its future destiny.

On Thursday, August 21, a little less than three months after leaving Bangkok, the *San Jacinto* anchored in the tiny harbor of Shimoda, the more worthless of the two poor ports which had been opened by the Perry Treaty.

## CHAPTER VIII

## THE ISLANDS OF ISOLATION

IN HIS search of the bookshops of New York for a library of reference books about Japan, the most recent publication Harris could find was the huge "History of Japan" by the Westphalian scholar and traveler, Engelbrecht Kaempfer, written about 1690 and published thirty years later. Until Perry's coming nothing of importance had been added to the knowledge of the outside world about this mysterious country. No one had been allowed to visit it except the Dutch and Chinese traders, and they were so rigidly restricted that they were virtual prisoners.

Although these restrictions were in effect when Kaempfer collected the material for his book, he was fortunate in obtaining entrance to the country as a physician attached to the Dutch trading post at Nagasaki. He remained there two years, made the humiliating pilgrimage to Yedo as "barbarian tribute bearer" and by persistence and devious methods secured a great deal of information which was usually denied foreigners. His book, on which Harris had to depend for much of his information, was surprisingly complete and accurate considering the difficulties under which the author worked. Harris did not have the benefit of the voluminous and verbose report of the Perry expedition for it was then in the hands of the printer.

At the time Perry visited Japan the Dutch had profited from their trade monopoly for about 230 years, having gained it after more than a half century of competition with the English, Spanish and Portuguese. The latter were first in the field and were the most strongly entrenched. In 1542 the Portuguese, in the course of their globe-circling voyages of adventure, evangelism, trade and conquest, had discovered Japan. The discovery was an accident as the Portuguese navigators were blown off their course by a typhoon while on their way from Macao to Siam—which was in exactly the opposite direction. The refugees made friends with the natives by teaching them the use of firearms—the West's first contribution to the education of Japan. The Japanese were eager to trade with them and welcomed the priests, who soon followed. For almost a hundred years the Portuguese played an active and often troublesome part in the affairs of the country. The trade between Japanese ports and the Portuguese colony of Macao proved tremendously profitable. The residents of Macao boasted that in a few years the city would be so rich that only gold would be used and silver would be looked on as of no value. The wealth brought to the colony by the Japanese trade was signalized by the building of a great cathedral whose ruined facade still stands as the principal landmark of Macao.

Work of the missionaries also flourished under the leadership of St. Francis Xavier. Portuguese Jesuits had penetrated to many strange parts of the heathen world, but in no other place had they met with such success. The annual reports which were sent to Rome told an amazing story of the progress with converts numbered first by the hundreds, then by the thousands, then by the tens of thousands, and later by the hundreds of thousands. Converts were not added as individuals but as groups of families or entire clans. Feudal lords who embraced Christianity ordered their retainers to

92

follow their example and thus thousands became nominal Christians at the nod of their local ruler. Other powerful feudal lords, while they made no pretense of becoming Christians themselves, encouraged their followers to embrace the strange new faith.

While undoubtedly a certain element of sincerity accompanied this endorsement of Christianity by the feudal lords, it is more than a coincidence that most of those who encouraged the Jesuits controlled ports which would be enriched by foreign trade. In the minds of the Japanese as well as the Portuguese, Christianity and foreign trade went hand in hand, one supporting the other. Where the priests were allowed to settle, ships and traders followed. The feudal lords who promoted trade by encouraging Christianity immediately found their fiefs enriched and many new avenues of taxation open to them. Nagasaki, which was one of the first centers of missionary effort, had been nothing but a small fishing village with a population of not more than a few thousand. But as a center of missionary effort, and a port of call for Portuguese ships, it grew in a few years to a city of 30,000 inhabitants, most of whom were Christians.

The encroachments of the Buddhist monasteries provided another reason for encouraging Christianity, which was looked on as a means of breaking the Buddhist power. The fact that no taxes were levied on church property had given the Buddhist orders an opportunity to increase their wealth and power which they were not slow to seize. Peasant landowners who were heavily taxed by the feudal lords found that they could make advantageous deals with the Buddhist monasteries by giving them their land and taking in return a freehold title at an annual rental which amounted to less than the former taxes.

The result was that the many monastic establishments constantly grew in wealth and power at the expense of the feudal lords and some of the monasteries maintained huge fortified castles with thousands of armed troops, who defied the lords. One of the most powerful of the sects into which Buddhism was divided had abolished the vows of celibacy and allowed its priests to marry, with the result that the office of abbot became hereditary and the families of abbots became more powerful than some of the feudal families. If the development had not been checked, the Buddhists of Japan would doubtless have become as powerful as their co-religionists in Thibet. The spread of Christianity provided this check and so for the moment served the political purpose of the feudal lords.

The Buddhists were quick to accept the challenge provided by the presence of the Jesuits, and the latter in self-defense were compelled to organize their adherents along military lines, a move in which they were encouraged and assisted by the feudal lords. So one religious power was merely replaced with another, and soon the lords became convinced that by encouraging the Christians in order to combat Buddhism they had introduced a new and greater danger. While the Buddhists were their own countrymen and offered nothing more serious than local revolts, the Christians were led by foreign priests who might be plotting the conquest of the country. Evidence of several plots of this nature was believed to have been discovered. The Portuguese traders and missionaries were followed by the Spaniards, and the Spanish Franciscans and Portuguese Jesuits were equally bitter and unscrupulous in the charges they hurled at each other. English and Dutch traders also came to Japan but brought no priests with them. Each na-

The new colony of Hongkong at the time of Harris' residence there

Malden Fort which faced the guns of Perry's fleet.

tion spread scandalous and malicious stories about the other three. The Dutch doubtless had a great deal to say about the Inquisition.

With the rapid increase in the number of ships calling at her ports, the Japanese rulers decided that the foreign priests must be driven out of the country and they were ordered expelled in a series of edicts which increased in severity as the first ones were evaded or ignored. The first of the many anti-Christian edicts was promulgated in 1578. Others followed, culminating sixty years later in a huge massacre of Christians; all who could be found were killed. In order that the "wicked sect" be given no opportunity to rise again, men, women and children were required to go through the form of trampling on the cross. No matter how skeptically one may question the methods by which Christianity was introduced into Japan there can be no doubt about the faith of the converts. Many of them heroically gave up their lives rather than renounce their faith. Others constructed secret chapels and generation after generation, at the risk of their lives, continued to practice the Christian rites.

With the expulsion of the priests, orders were given that any Portuguese ship coming to Japan be burned, the cargo destroyed and all on board executed. An unarmed delegation of Portuguese dignitaries came from Macao to plead for a revision of this cruel order but were made its first victims. All were executed except a couple of servants who were allowed to return to tell the tragic story. Further edicts added to the isolation of the country. No Japanese subject was to be allowed to go abroad, under pain of death, and no ship was to be built large enough to sail as far as the China Coast. The prohibition of foreign trade fell on all countries, but the Dutch, after being barred for a few years, were allowed, under severe and humiliating restrictions, to send one ship a year to Nagasaki. The traders were virtual prisoners for they were confined to the island of Deshima in Nagasaki Harbor. As this tiny island was partly artificial construction, the Japanese comforted themselves with the pretention that it was not actually a part of the soil of Japan. The rights of the Dutch were not confirmed by a treaty or agreement of any sort, and they remained in Japan on sufferance, for their privileges might have been ended at any moment. Portuguese, Spanish, and English traders who had been driven out of Japan promptly said that they had been denied the privilege of trade because they refused to repudiate their religion and trample on the cross, but that the Dutch did not hesitate to accept these humiliating conditions.

It is a curious fact that during the two centuries and more of Dutch monopoly, the only other ships which were peacefully received in Japan were of American ownership. During the war between England and Holland which marked the close of the 18th century the blockade of the English fleet was so complete that the Dutch did not dare dispatch their own ships from Batavia to Nagasaki and for four years the trade was carried on by American ships chartered by the Dutch company. The first of these voyages was made in 1798 by the *Eliza* of New York, followed at annual intervals by the *Franklin* of Boston, the *Massachusetts* of Boston and the *Margaret* of Salem. The visits of these four New England ships aroused a great deal of interest both in America and Japan and it is probable this was one of the reasons that the opening of Japan to trade became one of the early aims of the American Department of State.

With the end of the war with England the Dutch ships resumed the annual voyage to Nagasaki; and although venturesome traders of several nationalities attempted to establish themselves in the country and a number of ships were wrecked on its shores, no ships except the Dutch were allowed to remain in Japanese ports until the arrival of Perry's fleet in 1853. Several attempts were made by both America and England to open diplomatic negotiations with the Japanese, but the emissaries received no encouragement.

The development of the whaling industry by American ships had focused attention on the desirability of opening a few ports of Japan as places where the whaling ships could spend the winter or could anchor for repairs and secure water and provisions. A number of unsuccessful attempts were made to open negotiations. Roberts, who had negotiated the treaty with Siam, was commissioned to make a treaty with Japan but could not visit the country because he was out of funds. Elaborate preparations were made for this diplomatic effort and presents provided for the emperor included a repeating gold watch with a chain eight feet long. Traveling expenses were finally sent to Roberts but he died in Macao soon afterward. Commodore Biddle was commissioned to negotiate a treaty and went to Japan in a gunboat, only to be ordered away. The written reply given him by the Japanese officials was studiedly insulting and the commodore was given a blow or a shove by a Japanese soldier. Although the Japanese apologized for this incident and promised to punish the soldier, they took full advantage of it as an opportunity to discredit Americans. In distant Canton Americans heard how a Japanese soldier had

97

insulted an American commodore who was too cowardly to defend his honor.

In the meantime a long list of grievances had been suffered by American sailors from the whaling vessels shipwrecked on the coast of Japan. All were imprisoned and cruelly treated before being handed over to the Dutch at Nagasaki. A few died of exposure. American church members read with horror that all were compelled to spit on the cross.

The annexation of California, the discovery of gold and the development of steam navigation provided a new reason for the opening of ports where coal could be procured to replenish the bunkers for the long voyages across the Pacific. Because of the thriving whaling industry and the projected development of trans-Pacific steam navigation, America's interest in the opening of Japan was paramount. While other nations were interested solely in trade, America was interested principally in navigation and quite appropriately entrusted the negotiations with Japan to a distinguished naval officer.

Commodore Perry did not desire the task of negotiating a treaty with Japan, was very reluctant about accepting the commission, so as one of the terms of acceptance he was given practically a free hand in the arrangements. The letter of instructions which had been prepared by Daniel Webster, Secretary of State, was not entirely to his liking and the illness of Webster gave him an opportunity to write his own instructions, which were submitted to the State Department for approval. Webster's letter had ignored the cruelties to shipwrecked sailors, had been friendly to the point of timidity. Perry's instructions to himself were strong even after they had been toned down by the State Department. The Japanese people were described as "weak and semi-barbarous" and their treatment of shipwrecked sailors was described as bringing them into the category of nations which "may justly be considered the common enemy of mankind."

The instructions were to the effect that he was to use every possible argument to secure humane treatment for sailors, the opening of one or more ports to trade, and the right to purchase coal. If arguments proved unavailing, then he was to

change his tone and inform them in the most unequivocal terms that it is the determination of this government to insist that hereafter all citizens or vessels of the United States that may be wrecked on their coasts or driven by stress of weather into their harbors shall . . . be treated with humanity; and that if any acts of cruelty should hereafter be practised upon citizens of this country, whether by the government or the inhabitants of Japan, they shall be severely chastised.

He was to be accompanied by a strong fleet which President Fillmore referred to as a "persuader." However, he was cautioned against any acts of violence or any use of force except in self-defense "or to resent an act of personal violence offered to himself or to one of his officers."

Perry's arrival in the Bay of Yedo, July 8, 1853, in the first steam squadron the Japanese had ever seen, the decks cleared for action, the guns menacingly pointed at the comic-opera ports, threw the capitol into a panic. At night beacon fires flared from every hilltop and inadequately armed troops were moved in from the provinces. But under the iron rule of the Tokugawa Shogunate, the country had been at peace for more than a hundred years and the antiquated military machine was disorganized and useless.

99

There was a futile show of military strength but not a threatening gesture. After presenting his demands Perry sailed away, to return early the following year for the reply of the Japanese, this time accompanied by a fleet of ten vessels and a force numbering more than 2000. On his second visit Perry was not quite so independent as on the first. Pierce had succeeded Fillmore as President. The Washington authorities were disturbed by the truculent tone of Perry's dispatches and he had been sent a warning letter pointing out that he was to negotiate peacefully. In the meantime the Japanese government had decided to make the best terms possible with the American commodore and this decision was strengthened by the presence of the greatly augmented fleet. They would doubtless have given him much more than he got if he had asked for it.

The treaty which he concluded provided only for the opening to American ships of the ports of Shimoda and Hakodate where supplies could be purchased and coal stored, and for the residence of a Consul at Shimoda where he was to enjoy a status different in degree but not in kind from that of the Dutch at Nagasaki. He could secure living quarters and purchase provisions and supplies only through the Japanese officials and could not leave the port except with official permission. He could not go more than seven Japanese miles from a spot which was officially designated as the center of the port. The distance was set by Perry himself who had in mind the utmost limits a sailor on shore leave might travel and return to his ship on the same day.

The government had spared no expense in preparations for the expedition. No less than $30,000 was spent for charts alone and American sea-captains were interviewed as to the available ports. Yet the two selected have been described as "the worst in Japan." The port of Shimoda was so small and poor that it could not ordinarily supply the provisions for a single ship. Perry did not accept it without sending one of his captains on an inspection trip, and the report was favorable. But as the Japanese had plenty of notice that this inspection would be made, it is fair to presume that a great deal of window dressing was done. Perry later visited the place after the treaty had been signed and spent some time there. The amount of space devoted to a defense of Shimoda in the official account of the expedition indicates that he anticipated the criticism which soon followed. The arrangements for the purchase of ship stores were faulty for in the absence of any definite agreement as to exchange values, the American dollar was accepted at only one-third of its intrinsic worth.

The practical value of the treaty was small but the exclusive policy of Japan was broken down and the way prepared for the conclusion of a commercial treaty which would open the country to the trade of the world. The members of the expedition and especially the doughty commodore who headed it felt that they had every reason to be satisfied with their accomplishments. At the banquet which followed the signing of the treaty there was a feast of good fellowship at which the commodore became rhetorical and promised the Japanese many things which he fortunately did not put in writing.

## CHAPTER IX

## JAPAN'S UNWELCOME GUEST

THE arrival of the *San Jacinto* in Japan was enlivened by an incident that appeared to be very encouraging. With his typical methodical carefulness about everything connected with ships and the sea Commodore Perry had examined some of the local Japanese fishermen and selected three of them as licensed pilots with authority to conduct American ships into the harbor. Licenses were drawn up for them in the English and Dutch languages, printed on the press which comprised a part of the expedition equipment, signed by Flag Lieutenant Silas Bent and countersigned by the commodore. Each of the three pilots was then presented with a fine new overcoat and an American flag. The pilotage fees, based on fees for similar services in America, were so absurdly high that one ship a month would have kept all three pilots in luxury. When Harris arrived they had been waiting more than two years for an opportunity to earn these fees. As soon as the nationality of the *San Jacinto* could be distinguished one of them came out in his little boat, an American flag flying at the bow.

It was not only the first time a pilot boat in Japan had displayed the American flag, it was the first time in several centuries that any but a Dutch boat had been piloted into a Japanese harbor. The pilot could not give sailing directions in English but by a wave of his hand indicated that the frigate was to go to port or to starboard or straight ahead.

With the help of these gestures the *San Jacinto* reached anchorage without difficulty. The fact that a Japanese pilot with an American license had brought the ship into port appeared to Harris to indicate that there was smooth sailing ahead. But his hopes were false, for his welcome to Japan began and ended with the appearance of the pilot boat.

Three local officials with Dutch-speaking interpreters soon came on board and Mr. Heusken had his first painful experience in attempting to understand and interpret the peculiar language which the Japanese had picked up from the Dutch sailors at Nagasaki and supplemented by a study of Dutch books. The officials were solicitous about the health of the American official, curious about the length of the voyage and punctilious about the hospitality they had promised Commodore Perry to extend to American ships, for they volunteered the information that they would supply water and provisions. But when asked what provisions they could supply, they declined to commit themselves and said that "the Governor would answer."

This was also the reply when Harris asked whether or not a house had been prepared for him. They seized on this mention of his residence as an opportunity to discourage the idea of attempting to live in Shimoda by saying that it had always been a very poor place and was now even more poverty stricken than in the past, having suffered severely from the earthquake and tidal wave which had occurred two years previously. They did not add that this disaster, the worst in the history of the little fishing village, had followed so soon after the visit of Commodore Perry that superstitious Japanese looked on it as a divine reprimand and a warning to keep foreigners off their sacred soil. The tidal wave, which was thirty feet high, had come in and receded four times, each time adding to the destruction and loss of life. The fact that the wave had wrecked the Russian frigate *Diana* and had scoured the tiny harbor so thoroughly that there was no holding ground for the anchors of ships seemed to the Japanese convincing indication of the divine will. They did not exaggerate in the least when they described Shimoda as a poor place. It was nothing more than a small fishing village with a population of a few thousand, no wealth and no trade or industries of any kind.

Later in the afternoon the officials returned, but they did not bring a reply to the letter Harris had sent to the Governor as it was being translated. They said that the two letters he had written to officials at Yedo,* the capital, had been dispatched and would reach there in five days. Considering that the distance was less than a hundred miles, Harris found this information very surprising. It was only the first of many surprising pieces of information he was to receive when the officials found it to their interest to mislead him. They did inform Harris that the Governor would receive him at one o'clock the following afternoon. "The interpreters were in constant trepidation and fear, and large drops of perspiration stood on their foreheads, while every word of question and answer was written by two of the party."

On this visit the Japanese officials learned that Commodore Armstrong was unwell and when they went ashore and informed the governor he seized on this as a pretext for delay. The officials were on hand the following morning with inquiries about the health of the commodore and

* Yedo was the ancient name of the modern city of Tokyo. The present name was adopted in 1868 when the Emperor of Japan was restored to power and moved his court from the ancient seat in Kyoto.

104

the suggestion that owing to this unfortunate illness the proposed official call on the governor be postponed. In order to make the proposal for the postponement all the more convincing they said the governor was also unwell and so would be unable to keep his engagement for that afternoon. Harris, who was suspicious and on his guard, trapped them into some illuminating statements and found that it was their plan to delay his visit until the commodore was well enough to go with him. They would then be able to deny having received him as the American consular representative but could say that he had visited the governor solely as one of the commodore's suite.

In the interval following the Perry Treaty opposition to the opening of Japan to foreigners had increased and official policy now concentrated on efforts to avoid complying with the treaty provisions. The arrival of Harris to take up his residence in Shimoda was the first concrete evidence of the treaty obligations and the Japanese were determined to do everything in their power to compel him to leave.

Harris had anticipated the proposal to postpone his visit and was ready with his reply. He said:

This was a matter concerning the dignity of my government, that the Governor should write to me excusing himself on account of illness, and that I would send that letter to my government, and leave it for adjustment. This proposition greatly embarrassed them. The Governor was sick, therefore no letter was required. I insisted. They then offered to write to that effect themselves; this I declined. I finally closed the discussion by saying that if the Governor wrote his excuse to me before noon of tomorrow, I would be satisfied, but that otherwise I should come on shore tomorrow at one o'clock to visit him.

Having thoroughly impressed the Japanese by his firmness and shown that he as well as they could quote rules of etiquette to fit the occasion, Harris did not insist any further about the letter from the Governor and it was finally arranged that he would pay the call on Monday instead of Saturday.

While the official welcome to the American Consul-General left a great deal to be desired there was nothing half-hearted about the way the Japanese tradesmen welcomed the officers and crew of the *San Jacinto*. The day after the arrival of the frigate they hastily set up a bazaar adjacent to the Gaiyosho or town hall, where the officers and men bought lacquer ware, articles ornamented with mother-of-pearl and other strange trinkets of the sort the Japanese had been manufacturing for centuries to supply the Dutch trade. To the unsophisticated taste of the officers and crew, these articles appeared to be of fine workmanship and exceptionally cheap, but Harris who was familiar with the superior products of the Chinese and the treasures of the shops on the China Coast, found little merit in them. He thought the prices were outrageously high and made few purchases himself. All the booths in the bazaar were under strict official regulation and payment for purchases was made not to the shopkeepers themselves but to government cashiers.

The Japanese officials had professed ignorance as to whether or not a place of residence was prepared for Harris, but from unofficial quarters he learned that the Rioshen temple had been tentatively set aside for his use. He paid it a private visit and found it "isolated, and the approach through the narrow and crooked alleys of a poor fishing village." This first visit to the village which was to be his home was not encouraging. All Japanese fishing villages are poor and unattractive and this was one of the worst. An open sewer ran through the principal street and at low tide the foreshore was littered with half-decayed garbage which had not been swept out to sea. The houses were all of thatch, the roofs covered with mud. There were no chimneys and the insides of the houses were covered with soot from the kitchen fires. There was no market place and the few food shops displayed nothing that would be familiar to an American.

In spite of the fact that he had told them he would receive no visitors on Sundays the Japanese officials called, saying their business was very urgent. But they were given no opportunity to discuss it, as Harris remained in his cabin while Heusken talked to them on deck. They insisted that when Perry was in Japan he made no difference about Sundays. This statement was not correct, for Perry had been as rigid as Harris about Sabbath observance. Harris did take advantage of this opportunity to make it plain that his visit to the Governor the following day would be an official call as Consul-General and that he would not be accompanied by the commodore. The latter's illness had, in fact, fitted in very opportunely with his plan to establish himself in Japan and compel the Japanese to recognize his official status without the aid or support of armed force as represented by the navy. On Monday the officials were on hand early to confirm the engagement with the Governor and to assure Harris that everything was in readiness for the interview at ten o'clock.

The departure of Harris from the ship was made as impressive as possible. Three boatloads of officers and men first went ashore and lined up as a guard of honor at the landing place. Then as a fourth boat cast off with the

Consul-General, the hills surrounding the shores of Shimoda roared with a salute of thirteen guns. Pushing their way through a curious but orderly crowd of natives, Harris and his party reached the office of the Governor who had apparently made a very quick recovery. After the conventional inquiries about his visitor's health and the length of the voyage, the Governor suggested that they might get down to business at once. But here Harris scored again in the matter of ceremonial etiquette, for he said this was only a visit of ceremony and it would not be good breeding to discuss business. Refreshments were served and polite gossip exchanged for two hours, at the end of which time an engagement was made for another interview at the same hour the following day. A number of feudal lords were intensely interested in the negotiations, for in the two hours that the interview lasted every word was taken down by no less than seven different scribes. In this as in all subsequent interviews with Japanese officials three languages were used and a conversation between two people was participated in by four. Harris spoke in English and his remarks were translated into Dutch by Heusken for the benefit of the interpreter, who then translated them into Japanese. The replies came back over the same tedious route.

At this first business meeting the determined efforts to postpone the original engagement were explained by the presence of Moriyama, a silky and subservient individual who was introduced as a new interpreter, an employee of the newly created Ministry of Foreign Affairs. He had hastened down from Yedo to help the municipal governors induce the unwelcome diplomat to return to America. Harris had been told that it would take five days for his letters to reach Yedo, but in less than that time it had been possible to summon this official. Although his rank was only that of chief interpreter, Moriyama was actually the most experienced diplomat in Japan. For ten years he had attended to all the negotiations with the Dutch at Nagasaki and he had acted as interpreter for the commissioners who dealt with Perry. He was one of the very few Japanese who spoke English, though he was careful to conceal this fact from Americans and so was able to pick up a lot of useful information.

The business interview on Tuesday consumed three very unsatisfactory hours. The one idea in the minds of the Japanese was to induce Harris to return to America. They said that they understood that a Consul was to be appointed only if *both* nations desired it. That actually was the way the Japanese text of the Perry Treaty read, either because of a mistake in the translation or a wilful change. Moriyama was probably the only person who knew why the text of the two versions of the treaty did not agree for he had written the Japanese text and Perry had signed it without having it checked by his interpreters. That was not the only change that had been made in the Perry Treaty. The Chinese and Dutch copies provided that the treaty would be ratified within eighteen months, but the Japanese text read "after eighteen months."

However, the Governors did not confine themselves to this argument but used every plea they could think of. They understood that a Consul would be sent only when some difficulty arose and none had arisen. Shimoda was a poor place and there was no suitable residence. Yedo had also been devastated by an earthquake and no quarters could be provided for a Consul there. Didn't Harris think it would be a good idea to go away and come back in about a year? As fast as Harris politely but firmly gave a negative reply to one suggestion they went on to another and then came back to the old ones again, repeating them with or without modification. It was the age-old method of wearing out an opponent—the same method the statesmen of Siam had tried with such little success. At the end of three hours Harris was just as firm in his refusals as at first and gave no hint that he was either impatient or tired. It was the Japanese officials who finally asked that the conference adjourn for a day to give them time to consult.

Harris agreed to this and as soon as the conference was over he made a gesture which was more convincing to the Japanese than weeks of argument would have been. He gave an order to a Japanese lumber dealer for spars for his consular flagstaff. The main spar was probably the largest that had ever been ordered in Shimoda—so large the lumber dealer could not supply it out of stock but had to send workmen to the hills to cut it. We may be sure that within an hour everyone in Shimoda had heard about this and that the news was being relayed to the capital.

At the conference the following day neither the Governor nor the Vice-Governor was present. There were ten people in the official reception rooms including Moriyama, who explained that the Governor had suffered from a headache the night before and they had been unable to consult with him; the Vice-Governor also was sick. However, Moriyama had without the aid of these colleagues thought up a new reason why Harris should not be received. The Perry Treaty provided for the residence of a Consul but nothing was said about a Consul-General. Harris was a Consul-General, not a Consul, therefore he

American gunboats in the small harbor of Shimoda

Chief interpreter Moriyama *(left)* and assistant

had no standing under the terms of the treaty. Harris did not bother to discuss this issue but expressed his surprise that the Vice-Governor should break his engagement and said that he would go on board to consult with Commodore Armstrong about going up the bay to Yedo to get satisfaction for the lack of respect he was being shown.

Moriyama then disclosed his real identity, confirming what Harris had suspected from the first. He was not only the official interpreter but also a high ranking official of Yedo who had actually come down to conduct the negotiations. He was in fact of even higher rank than the Governor of Shimoda. Harris insisted that his relations were only with the Governor and the Vice-Governor, that he would talk to no one else unless he went to Yedo to talk to the officials there. Moriyama at once promised to have the Vice-Governor on hand the following morning. Harris declined to be satisfied with this. The Vice-Governor had broken his appointment and he, Harris, would not make another one until he had received an explanation or an apology. He would go on board the steamer and wait for a letter from the Governor or Vice-Governor stating "whether they would receive me in Shimoda or not, and whether they would assign me a house to reside in; that I desired this letter to be sent to me either today or tomorrow."

The following morning the Vice-Governor, Moriyama and many others came on board the *San Jacinto*. The Vice-Governor either forgot that he was seriously ill the previous day or the illness had been invented by Moriyama. He explained his absence by saying that Moriyama was of higher rank than himself and had full authority to act. He also forgot his earlier objections to receiving Harris

111

under any circumstances; now he was anxious for the American to move at once into the Rioshen temple which he insisted had been built "solely for the reception of strangers of distinction who came to Shimoda." The place was not all that it should be but they would fix it up and he hoped it would be accepted as a temporary residence until another could be built. Harris grumbled that the temple was in a suburb of Shimoda rather than in the town itself, but agreed to accept it as a temporary residence, and in order to settle this matter at once asked that two large boats be sent to the *San Jacinto* the same afternoon to take his belongings to his new quarters.

## CHAPTER X

# REINFORCEMENTS ARRIVE FROM YEDO

THE question of Harris' reception as Consul-General and his residence in Shimoda appeared to have been settled to his satisfaction, so when the Governor invited him to pay another call he did not anticipate further argument. He assumed that this call would mend and cement the friendly relations which had been so near the breaking point and erase all memory of sharp words spoken. Commodore Armstrong was now completely recovered and able to pay his first visit to the Governor. His illness had been opportune for Harris, whose plan it was to carry on negotiations without a hint of coercion. He had for some reason assumed that this was understood and agreed on between the commodore and himself, but apparently not; for when inquiries were made about the commodore's health the latter volunteered the information that if he had not been sick he would have been present at the first interview. The Japanese were quick to note that this contradicted what Harris had told them, they began to doubt whether he was in fact independent of the commodore.

On their arrival at the town hall Harris was surprised to meet two new officials, a new Governor and Vice-Governor who had just arrived from Yedo complaining that they were worn out by the long journey. Moriyama blandly explained that according to the laws of the country two sets of provincial officials alternated in serving at their official posts and residing at Yedo. This was in fact the arrangement by which the Shogun kept control of the local daimyos. While one set of officials remained in the country other members of the family were kept at Yedo as hostages. Each six months the officials on duty returned to Yedo and the hostages were released to take up their official posts. Thus the arrival of new Governors was a matter of regular routine. But the change at this time was too opportune for the Japanese authorities to have been a mere coincidence. The two Governors whom Harris had met had done their best to prevent his assuming his post as Consul-General but had failed; and now the arrival of the new Governors gave, it was hoped, an opportunity to reopen the whole question. Harris did not like the looks of the new Governor. He had a dark and sullen look "like a bandog" and Harris was afraid he would have trouble with him. He did have plenty of trouble with the man, as with all other Japanese officials, but they later became the best of friends.

The old Governor did not return to Yedo and neither did Moriyama. Both remained in the little fishing village to attend to the foreign relations of Japan which for the moment were concentrated in the person of Townsend Harris. The only times they left the place were for hurried visits to Yedo to consult with the Council of State and receive fresh instructions.

The new Governors had to go through the routine of inquiries about the health of President Pierce, the Consul-General, the commodore and the officers of the ship. When this was over they immediately plunged into the business at hand, frequently consulting a document which apparently consisted of written instructions prepared by the officials at Yedo. The first question was: what secret reasons had brought Harris to Japan? Harris replied that he knew nothing about the secret plans of his government. All he knew was that he had been appointed Consul-General in accordance with the rights provided for in the treaty. Then they ran over the old objections and arguments which had been worn threadbare by the first Governors and when these had been exhausted with no effect they politely asked Harris if he would not please return to America.

On his refusal they turned to Commodore Armstrong and asked him if he did not have the power to take the Consul-General away. The commodore replied that as he was under military orders he had no power to do anything but carry out those orders—which were to bring the Consul-General to Shimoda and leave him there. Then, they asked, would he take a letter to the government of the United States explaining their objections to the presence of the Consul-General and asking for his recall? The commodore replied that he would, of course, take any communication they entrusted to him, but it would have to come through the Consul-General. They next wanted to know if the commodore would write his government explaining why the Japanese refused to receive the Consul-General.

The officials made particular inquiries about the duties and powers of a Consul, a point on which Commodore Perry had been evasive to the point of actual deception. In fact he had pictured to the Japanese a consular official who would be a kind of glorified police sergeant detailed to help the Japanese discipline unruly American sailors and collect debts owed them by the Americans. Perry had explained:

I could only induce the commissioners to agree to this article by endeavoring to convince them that it would save the Japanese government much trouble if an American agent were to reside at one or both of the ports opened by the treaty, to whom complaints might be made of any mal-practice on the part of United States citizens who might be within the Japanese dominions.

He had also given the Japanese every reason to believe that a Consul might not be sent, for he told them that one would not be appointed until the government "considered it necessary." The treaty stipulated that a Consul was not to be appointed for eighteen months; President Pierce had not waited that long before appointing the historian Brodhead.

Harris was genuinely surprised at the course the conversation was taking. This was his first intimation that in spite of the promises made by the old Governors they still intended to refuse to receive him. He protested that his was a ceremonial visit, the first call of the commodore and his first meeting with the new Governors, and he had not come prepared to reopen the old negotiations. But the Governors tossed aside these considerations of etiquette and the arguments continued until lunch was served, when the old as well as the new Governors retired for a consultation. Commodore Armstrong then returned to the *San Jacinto* with the principal member of his staff, a gesture indicating that the negotiations were entirely in the hands of the Consul-General.

Apparently at their luncheon-time conference the Japanese officials came to the conclusion that their bluffing tactics would not work for they adopted a new and more conciliatory tone.

They apologized for delaying and wasting so much time in trivial questions; but their excuse was their want of knowledge of such matters. That it was a new thing, etc., etc. They asked me if I had any new negotiations to propose. I answered none at that time. Did I intend to make new negotiations about sailors who were shipwrecked, or should I change the place of the consulate without giving notice to them? I answered, "No." They then begged me again to write to my government the strong objections they had to receiving a Consul at this time, stating that they had opened Shimoda to the Dutch and Russians, and that they would send a Consul here as soon as they knew I was received here (this was news). I replied that I could not write any formal letter; that if I did, it would not be attended to on such a point; that I should, as a matter of course, give my government an account of all that had occurred here, but they might be sure it would not elicit any reply; that, if they wanted to communicate with the government of the United States, let their Minister of Foreign Affairs write a letter, and he might depend on receiving a speedy answer.

In the meantime the boats which had been ordered to take off the Consul-General's baggage and stores had arrived at the *San Jacinto*, and the spars for the flagstaff were also on deck being shaped by the carpenter. Before the afternoon was ended all of the furniture, supplies and some of the heavy baggage had been sent off.

At the conclusion of the interview the new officials begged Harris not to be offended with them as they were acting under orders and had no choice but to carry out their instructions. They said the business was all strange to them and perhaps appeared more alarming than it really was. It was obvious that they had been sent with instructions to use every method possible to induce Harris to go away, and having used up their whole bag of tricks and failed they surrendered with at least a show of graciousness.

Harris did not know that Shimoda had been opened as a port to both the Russians and the Dutch until the Governor mentioned the fact. It explained, in part at least, the determined opposition to his establishing a residence there. Two treaties, which had followed hard upon Perry's compact, provided for the appointment of Consuls by the Dutch and Russians, and the Japanese knew that once they allowed Harris to land and set up his consular office they could not offer any objections, valid or invalid, to receiving the others. The Russian Treaty had been signed on January 26, 1855, the preliminary Dutch Treaty on November 6.

Opposition to intercourse with foreigners was growing steadily in Japan and there was a strong faction which hoped that in some way the provisions of the trade treaties might be circumvented. In the accomplishment of this objective the first thing to do was to prevent the landing of Harris and it was on this point that all energies were centered. While Harris thought that he was battling only for his own rights, as a representative of the United States government, he was in fact playing a much larger part, for he was the symbol of the West. Every ingenuous device the Japanese could think of had been thrown in his way and they thought of many more in the months which followed.

The Japanese protestations that they were ignorant of foreign ways and diplomatic usage constituted one of these naive devices. Their isolation had not kept them in ignorance of what was going on in the world. One of the reasons for allowing the Dutch and Chinese to continue their trade monopolies was to provide the officials at Yedo with news of events in Europe and Asia. How closely the Japanese kept in touch with European affairs was illustrated in 1683 when the British East India Company attempted to reopen trade at Nagasaki; according to the British emissary, the Japanese reply was "that since our King (Charles II) was married with the daughter of Portugal, their enemy, they could not admit us to have trade and for no other reason." Moriyama's pleas of ignorance were especially absurd. He was, compared to Harris, a veteran diplomat. As chief interpreter at the foreign office he was one of its most important officials and had played a major part in all negotiations with foreigners. These protestations were of course designed to flatter and to throw the foreigner off his guard. There were never any manifestations of ignorance that did not work to the advantage of the Japanese themselves or serve as an excuse for deliberate breaches of etiquette.

This had been a Blue Monday for Harris but before it ended everything was serene and the Japanese officials were invited to be his guests on board the *San Jacinto* the following day. It turned out to be a merry party; the first since his arrival that had not been marked by disputes which would have become acrimonious but for the unfailing patience and urbanity of the American envoy. At this party there was no opportunity for disputes. There was no further talk of treaty rights, no busy secretaries writing down every word that was said to be forwarded to some distant and suspicious daimyo. Every member of the ship's company helped to entertain the visitors. The band played and the marines were put through their paces. A salute was fired as the Governor had expressed a desire to see as well as hear one. When the food was brought on the Americans

119

noted that the tenets of Buddhism did not in any way discourage their guests' consumption of meat. They "ate ham, tongue, cold chicken, lobster salad, hard bread, soft bread and cakes," and in generous quantities. This was no time for austerity. They used liberal quantities of mustard and olive oil but in unorthodox ways.

The ship's canteen was thrown open and, except for Moriyama, they tasted, probably for the first time, ale, champagne, white wine and brandy. The lightest of these beverages was heady stuff compared to their light *sake* but this was something the Japanese did not know and have not yet learned. They stood not on the order of their drinking but mixed all their drinks together, just as they had eaten cake with lobster salad and mustard on bread. Soon the serious world was replaced by a gay one. The officials who had been so unbending shouted and laughed and played practical jokes—such as putting mustard in each other's hair.

When they could eat no more, they wrapped up neat little parcels of the food to take home with them. In Japan it was the custom for the host to provide his guests with parcels like this so that the enjoyment of the feast could be continued into another day. The Japanese saw no reason why they should forego this pleasure just because the Americans were not familiar with the etiquette prevailing on Japanese soil.

They were completely relaxed after their arduous official duties. In fact, between the cautious lines of Harris' journal and the slightly less restrained comments of the naval officers it is perfectly obvious that the Japanese guests got gloriously and enjoyably drunk.

## CHAPTER XI

# A BACHELOR HOUSEKEEPER IN JAPAN

THE day following this gay party Harris wrote a long report to Secretary Marcy and then moved over to his temple. He was somewhat disappointed that the *San Jacinto* carpenter had not been able to complete the flagstaff, probably because the party of Tuesday had interfered with his work. The erection of the flagstaff and the hoisting of the flag was a symbol to him. Not only was it the first consular flag to be seen on Japanese soil, it was a symbol of his personal triumph over Japanese opposition. He wanted the flag to fly at a height that would make it visible to boats coming into the harbor and also to all the countryside. In consequence he paid an outrageous price for the tallest spars he could find.

The flagstaff came on board Wednesday but too late to put up; the men from the *San Jacinto* came early the following morning, September 4, to erect it. This was not a simple job. The large lower spar had to be set in the ground and the smaller spar fixed in braces above it. Harris impatiently commented that the work was heavy and slow and that not enough men had been sent from the ship. All hands were busy on what was to the commodore the more important business of getting away from Japan. Having carried out his orders to deliver the Consul-General at Shimoda, Commodore Armstrong felt that his duty was done, and he was anxious to hurry away to the China Coast where there were other ships under his command and work which was more to the taste of a naval officer. The sailors were also anxious to get away and worked hurriedly and carelessly. One of the spars fell, breaking the crosstrees, and more men were sent for to help finish the job. It was not until half past two in the afternoon that the work was completed. As Harris recorded in his journal: "I hoist the first consular flag ever seen in this Empire. Grim reflections —ominous of change—undoubtedly the beginning of the end. Is it for the good of Japan?"

Harris may have been disappointed that Commodore Armstrong and the officers of the *San Jacinto* did not help him make a little ceremony out of this significant flag-raising, but he said nothing about it in his journal. The sailors who had erected the flagstaff did form a ring around it while he hoisted the flag, but that was all.

Then as soon as the party returned to the *San Jacinto*, she upped anchor and sailed away, dipping her flag in farewell; and the long exile of the Consul-General had begun. He had no one to talk to except Heusken and no companions but the Chinese servants. It was the first time in his life that he had not been surrounded by friends, for he made friends wherever he traveled. Here there was no opportunity for friendship; his associations were confined to the Japanese officials with whom he had always to be on guard. Even the atmosphere was unfriendly, in sharp contrast to the China Coast. There the democratic Chinese with easy-going ways would always answer a smile with a smile, and were always ready for a bit of friendly gossip. Here a smile or any other friendly advance received but one response—a stolid stare of indifference. Only the little girls were friendly, but exceedingly shy. It was a red letter day in Harris' life when one of them allowed him to pat her on the head. It was an event in her life also for she boasted of the incident seventy years later. But he was determined to establish relations with the Japanese on a basis of friendship and made his plans accordingly. In a long letter which he wrote to Secretary Marcy the day he moved into the temple he said:

I have deemed it prudent to let a few weeks elapse before I open to the Japanese the matters contained in your instructions. I wish to let the alarm occasioned by my arrival subside; to convince them by my quiet conduct of my friendly disposition; and by such friendly intercourse as I may have, establish a friendly feeling toward me.

Even if he had not decided to adopt this program of delay as a matter of policy he would soon have found it forced on him by the homely duties of setting up housekeeping. At the present day the foreigner who moves into a house in Japan finds the task of getting himself comfortably settled tedious and difficult, for Japanese do not use any of the furniture and utensils which are necessities in the foreign household. They can now be procured by diligent search but at that time they were entirely unknown. The shops of Shimoda were stocked only to fill the simple wants of the fishermen and contained nothing else.

The house was as devoid of furnishings as an empty freight car. There were no shelves, closets or tables. No one knew how to make tables or chairs and they had to be laboriously constructed under Harris' superintendence, from his own clumsy designs. Neither Heusken nor the Chinese servants were able to help him. He had brought a tailor with him from Hongkong but he had more need for a

Chinese carpenter. He was so busy with his housekeeping arrangements that he did not have time to take his customary walks, could not even attend the local village festival, although Heusken went and later told him all about it.

One can imagine the difficulties of this middle-aged bachelor, the first foreigner to set up his own household in the country. The usual helplessness of the unmarried man had been increased by his life on the China Coast where he had many well-trained servants to anticipate every want. There was no friendly and hospitable assistance from the Japanese. Indeed, they seemed to take a vicious delight in thwarting him in everything he attempted to do and in introducing him to strange customs of the country which appeared to have been especially designed to add to his discomfort and inconvenience.

After the market man had supplied him with a number of old roosters which were so tough that he could not eat them, he insisted that he wanted only hens or pullets. The market man's reply was that in Japan chickens were hatched in pairs, one hen and one rooster, and could only be sold in that way. It was a custom of the country. As for pullets, he was to learn what every other Western resident of the Orient has learned, that hens are never killed for the market until disease or old age has rendered them incapable of laying eggs. In an attempt to get chickens he could eat Harris bought live fowls and tried to fatten them, but after a few of them died he was afraid to kill and eat those which remained. When he complained of having been sold diseased chickens the officials explained that no others were available, as all the chickens in Shimoda had been stricken with disease. To every complaint the Japanese responded with apologies and expressions of regret and promises to investigate. But they did nothing to reduce the causes for complaint.

The first night Harris spent in the temple he could not sleep on account of the mosquitoes, which "were of enormous size." These were not the only insect pests. There was a noisy cricket which amused itself by imitations of a steam locomotive, and a "death's head" spider with legs extended more than five inches as it stood. Rats, large both in size and numbers, ran around the house as they do around all Japanese temples. Cockroaches later added to his burdens and at first he thought he had brought them from the *San Jacinto*. The Japanese officials probably told him that there were no cockroaches in Japan.

He had brought from Hongkong four pairs of pigeons and one of the first things he did on moving into the temple was to have a belfry converted into quarters for them. A cat killed the pigeons. At the same time weasels were killing the hens.

Not all of his troubles could be charged to the Japanese. The tailor who had lost all his money gambling in Macao for some unknown reason went on a strike and refused to do any work. He was homesick and frightened in these strange surroundings and adopted this method of forcing Harris to send him back home.

I gave him a serious lecture. Told him that if he expected to eat he must work; that I had the power of putting him in jail and causing him to be fed on very spare diet, and also might order him to be whipped every day; that I would give him until Monday to reflect which he would take—work, wages and good food—or prison, hunger and a whipping.

The tailor continued to be a thorn in his side, and Harris sent him back to Hongkong at the first opportunity.

It was apparent that the Chinese servants were not going to be as satisfactory as he had anticipated so he asked for two Japanese boys who could be trained. After a delay of four or five days he was told that the matter had been referred to Yedo. The day following a storm of unusual severity, Moriyama and his suite called to ask whether or not Harris had been frightened by the thunder. The official then brought up the subject of servants. There were no servants in Shimoda, he said. It would be necessary to write around to other places about them. Some time later they were provided, but the officials insisted that they could not live on the premises, they must return to their homes every night.

The second day the fine new flag was hoisted the wind whipped out the hem and frayed the bunting. The sealing wax which had been supplied by the State Department would not run but when lighted burned to the end like a splinter of pine. An iron safe Harris had bought in New York would not respond to the key and when Japanese mechanics managed to open it, it could not be locked again. The patent stove he had brought from home proved as unsatisfactory as the safe. The plates warped and cracked the first time it was lighted, provoking Harris' philosophical comment that he now had a smoky house but no scolding wife. As the stove was a contraption strange alike to the local Japanese and to his Chinese servants, he spent a great deal of time himself in attempts to repair it. In fact he did so much manual labor that on one visit of the Japanese officials he was able to show them his blistered hand, as proof that their neglect of his requests had put him to a lot of unnecessary labor.

He was not the only American the Japanese were trying

to discourage from making visits to the country. The first letter he received from Captain Bell of the *San Jacinto* was full of complaints about the poor quality of coal the Japanese had supplied. Harris wrote a report about the coal, just as he wrote reports about everything in Japan which might be of the slightest value to his government. In fact he did the work that would today be entrusted to a number of different governmental departments. He ran a complete weather observatory, recording four times a day the temperature, the barometric pressure and the direction of the winds. The present Department of Agriculture was then a neglected step-child of the Patent Office and for it he collected seeds of strange Japanese vegetables that he thought might be of interest to the American farmers. There were no idle moments.

Not content with annoying him, the Japanese picked on his Chinese servants. They went out for a walk and three policemen followed them. A shopkeeper refused to sell them any fruit and when they tried to get a drink of water from a well, a Japanese ran away with the dipper. The officials assured him that there was no fresh fruit in Shimoda, but when the Chinese cook reported having seen fine ripe grapes and persimmons in the market, he charged the officials with falsehood and they began to send him a daily supply of fruit. At this time Harris had been in Shimoda less than two weeks and, finding that polite insistence accomplished nothing, had already begun to pass the lie direct to the officials. When he found that they did not appear to mind he explained that in America to call a man a liar was considered a deadly insult. This explanation did not change the Japanese custom. They continued to lie to him and did not appear particularly perturbed when their lies were discovered. Truth was a precious commodity, not to be lightly bandied about but a courtesy reserved for friends.

At the first severe storm the house was shaken, a roof of the kitchen blew in and the flagstaff keeled over to an angle of 65°. No Japanese workman could be found to repair the flagstaff and it continued to look like the mast of a derelict ship until the crew of a Russian frigate straightened it several months later. The supply of grapes was cut off—according to the Japanese officials, the crop had been destroyed by the storm.

In the midst of these troubles Harris noted in his journal under the date of October 4, 1856: "I am fifty-two years old today. God grant that the short remainder of my life may be more usefully and honorably spent than the preceding and larger portion of it."

CHAPTER XII

# FROM HOUSEKEEPING TO DIPLOMACY

STORIES of the fanatical hatred in which Christianity was held by the Japanese, and of their demand that foreigners as well as natives trample on the cross or the picture of the Virgin Mary, had traveled farther and created a more profound impression than any other information about the country. There was about these tales a hint of witchcraft and the diabolical which both shocked and fascinated. Every shipwrecked sailor or other traveler had some new story to tell and nothing was lost in the telling. One American said he was exchanging autographs with a Japanese acquaintance and asked the latter to write his name in a prayer book. "He had dipped his camel's-hair pencil into his portable inkstand, passed the point through his lips, and was about to write when his eye rested upon the cross; he instantly shook his head, threw the book upon the table, nor could he be induced to touch it again."*

In his letter of instructions Secretary Marcy had urged Harris to provide in the Siam Treaty for some protection for the American missionaries who were living there with no rights or protection other than that afforded at the pleasure of the King, but had cautioned the Consul-General to be very careful about bringing this up with the Japanese authorities as he was afraid it might arouse their resentment and opposition to the more important matter of

* J. W. Spalding in *The Japan Expedition*, New York, 1855.

a trade treaty. Harris did tread cautiously, but as a regular church attendant and former Sunday School teacher he felt deeply this Japanese persecution of Christianity. Without actually raising the issue, he did provide the background for its discussion by making it clear that he would neither pay nor receive calls nor transact public business on the Sabbath; and with Mr. Heusken as both clerk and congregation he held services every Sunday, making no effort at either publicity or concealment.

He overlooked no opportunity to investigate the matter of persecutions. In his walks around Shimoda he found the small Russian cemetery where the sailors were buried who had drowned following the wrecking of the *Diana*. Plainly cut in the gravestones were the double crosses of the Greek Orthodox Church. Harris took this to "prove that the Japanese of the present day have not that excessive hatred of the cross that was said to animate them formerly." He put the matter to a further test by showing Moriyama a copy of Mitchell's Atlas, in which the frontispiece consisted of a colored engraving of the "Landing of Columbus" with a large and prominently displayed cross. This did not arouse any of the violent reactions which other travelers had described, for Moriyama looked at the picture attentively but said nothing.

Harris was quite correct in his assumption that the Japanese hatred of Christianity had cooled. It had been encouraged as a political measure, had served its purpose of helping to break the power of the Buddhists, and had been driven out when its continued growth created a new problem. But for about two centuries it had not been an issue, although Christian congregations had been maintained in secrecy. When shipwrecked sailors were compelled to trample on the cross, the always provocative Japanese police were merely taking advantage of an old regulation in order to humiliate the foreigner and discourage any further attempts to visit the country. The sight of Perry's huge armed force clearly indicated that foreigners could no longer be treated as trespassing barbarians and the old ordinance became a dead letter even though it had not been repealed. In fact, when Perry's second expedition was in Japan four of the marines died and all were buried with full Christian rites attended by Japanese officials. It is perhaps significant that after more than eighty years of unrestricted missionary effort and with intensive work by many societies, the number of Christians now in Japan is less than one-tenth the number claimed in 1584 when Christianity was encouraged as a political measure.

In the meantime all the problems of negotiating a new treaty which would provide for freedom of both religion and trade were submerged by the more immediate problem of securing a reasonable amount of personal liberty for himself—a problem rendered all the more difficult of solution because the Japanese themselves neither enjoyed personal liberty nor appeared to desire it. Every act of their lives—even the number of garments, the quality and style of the clothing they wore—was regulated by law, while in addition to these sumptuary regulations every Japanese was subject to the whim of his superior who held the absolute power of life or death. The subservient politeness which provided such a striking and outwardly pleasing characteristic of the race had its origin in the fear that some chance act might be displeasing to a superior and be punished by death. The social regimentation of the country was similar to that of Siam, for both had been modeled after the feudal period of China.

The Japanese formula for the reception and treatment of foreigners had been worked out for application to the Dutch at Deshima and this was the procedure they attempted to apply to Harris. The Dutch confined to the small island could not leave it without the permission and escort of the police officials who were quartered on the island with them, watching them as carefully as jailors guarding convicts. They could not deal with tradesmen or employees except through officials.

In their arrangements for the residence of Harris the Japanese officials duplicated these conditions as far as possible. The Perry Treaty had sanctioned the spirit of these restrictions by providing that the Americans could not travel more than seven Japanese miles from Shimoda and the Japanese assumed the right to make other restrictions. The phrasing of the Perry Treaty in fact made the restrictions appear as a privilege, for it stated that Americans were free to travel where they pleased—but within the seven mile limit. As no special provision had been made for the freedom of the Consul-General, this regulation also applied to him.

The Japanese officials first arranged that a number of policemen be quartered in the small temple itself, assuring Harris that this was necessary for his protection. When he indignantly refused to allow this intrusion on his privacy, the guards were quartered at his gateway. Here they cross-questioned every visitor, brow-beat the Chinese servants, and spied on Harris and Heusken even to the point of following them when they went for walks. Harris lived in a prison without walls—though the walls were very effectively supplied by the ever-vigilant police. When workmen, who were always chosen by the officials, were sent to attend to some simple repairs about the house one of the policemen was always at his elbow with the ostensible purpose of seeing that the work was done properly, but for the real purpose of seeing that there was no communication between Harris and the workman. He lived in isolation as complete as that of the Dutch at Deshima so far as his contact with the Japanese people was concerned.

All his contacts were through the Japanese officials. He was not allowed to employ his own Japanese servants or workmen nor could he or his Chinese butler or cook purchase any provisions or supplies. His shopping list was submitted to the Governors, who sent him what was required and later billed him at prices which proved to be considerably above the market rate. The officials had their own ideas as to what food he should eat, and while they failed to supply many things he had ordered they substituted others he did not want. Time after time his request for certain articles, which either Harris or his servants had seen in the shops of Shimoda, was met with the information that these articles could not be procured. The only food staple he had no difficulty securing was the sweet potato, which had been introduced by the Dutch and was a kind of culinary outcast, being eaten only by the lower classes. For more than two months he had sweet potatoes at every meal except tea and breakfast.

Aside from the fact that he had to pay very high prices for articles purchased through the Japanese officials, he had to settle for them at a ruinous rate of exchange. This introduced a pressing problem which had to be straightened out before foreign trade could be developed on any sound basis. The Perry Treaty provided that American money be accepted but omitted to establish a rate. The principal Japanese coin was the silver *ichibu* which was normally exchanged for about 1600 smaller coins, known as *seni*. The *seni* was a humble coin similar in appearance and value to the better known Chinese *cash*. The American dollar weighed three times as much as the *ichibu* and therefore should have been exchanged for about 4800 *seni*, but under the ratio of exchange established by the Japanese officials was exchanged at the same rate as the *ichibu*. This added a full 200 per cent to the cost of all provisions and supplies bought in Japan, including the supplies Harris bought for his own table. He was, in fact, the first to suffer from this careless provision of the Perry Treaty.

Perry had made no attempt to settle this important matter of exchange until his departure made necessary the payment of a number of accounts for supplies. Even then he did not enter into any negotiations himself but turned the problem over to two pursers who reported that the Japanese were unreasonable. And there the matter rested. The Japanese insisted that American coins should not be accepted as coins but as bullion, and under the same terms by which the officers of the Japanese mint enriched themselves. For the bullion they received they returned coins of approximately one-third the weight.

The Dutch had been doing business with the Japanese for more than two centuries, but the inequalities of Japanese exchange had never proved any hindrance to trade which was based on exchange of commodities. In fact at the time of Harris' arrival in Shimoda the Dutch were building several steamers for the Japanese; and they were to be paid for in Japanese produce—copper, wax, lacquer, and camphor; bullion to represent one-fifth of the purchase price. Dutch mechanics who had already arrived in Nagasaki were teaching the Japanese all the different branches of ship-building according to the European style.

Harris' protests to the Governors about this unfair exchange were met by the response that the question would have to be referred to Yedo. There the matter rested and no action was taken. The imperial mint was the very profitable perquisite of a group of Japanese nobles. Although this class affected to despise money, they could not be blind to the practical advantages of an arrangement whereby they could exchange one *ichibu* for one dollar, out of which they could make three *ichibus* by the simple process of recoining.

Confronted by these and many other problems calculated to provoke the most righteous man to anger, Harris registered and repeated his protests, verbally and in writing, but kept his peace and returned good for evil. His dispatches to the State Department contained no hint of the many petty annoyances and discomforts he suffered. He never deviated from the policy of friendliness he had promised Secretary Marcy he would follow. He met inhospitality with friendly advances and saw to it that in the balance sheet of social and diplomatic amenities the Japanese were always in debt to him. A few days after his arrival he told the Governor that he would hoist the consular flag on Japanese as well as American holidays and they provided him with a list. The flag was thereafter ceremonially hoisted on Japanese holidays even when the flagstaff stood at a dizzy and ludicrous angle because the officials would not provide workmen to repair it.

A well-stocked sideboard provided one of the most useful implements of his hospitality. Although he had foresworn drinking himself Harris was quick to see that the Japanese not only liked alcohol but were easily affected by it, especially as they drank whisky and brandy "neat" just as they drank their own light *sake*. With a few glasses of champagne, which they frequently mixed with whisky and gin, their stiffness disappeared and was succeeded by an exuberant alcoholic friendliness. As soon as he unpacked his stores Harris sent each of the two Governors "two five-pints of champagne, one quart of brandy, two quarts of whisky, one cherry bounce and one anisette." At this time the officials who received these gifts, which came from his own stores, were telling him that no fresh fruit was available. Drinks were always served when Japanese officials called and there is no doubt but that many of them went away with flushed faces and uncertain steps. After a few of these visits he recorded in his journal: "I may here remark that at all these visits, they readily drink all I offer them —wine, cordials, brandy, whisky, etc., and many of them drink more than enough."

The officials asked him all kinds of questions about the United States and other foreign countries to which he gave patient and truthful replies but he could get no satisfactory answers to such simple inquiries as what was the population of Yedo. "They said it was a large place; that there was such a large number of persons coming and going daily that it was out of their power to state the population." After months of residence in the country he still had to refer to Kaempfer's old history of Japan for information which could easily have been supplied by any Japanese official. He met their secretiveness about their own country by giving them books about the United States.

After weeks of discouragement there were some indica-

136

tions that his patience was being rewarded. The officials had not replied to his letter about the exchange at which the dollar would be accepted, but in the settlement of a small account he was given 4800 of the small copper coins, the number which he had been insisting constituted the correct exchange. About the same time he was able to write in his journal: "The Japanese officials are daily becoming more and more friendly and more open in their communications with me. I hope this will grow and lead to good results by and by."

Each day appeared much like the rest and there were no noticeable changes in the routine of life, but difficulties did disappear. His clumsy efforts finally brought to his lonely household a satisfactory amount of bachelor comfort. The pigeons the cat had killed were replaced. The replenished poultry-house was full of fruitful hens. One went broody and he set her with very successful results. The sow he brought from China farrowed. The faulty stove was still imperfect but provided heat for the chilly autumn evenings—except when the absent-minded Heusken got absorbed in a book and let the fire go out. The officious guards were still at his gate but not quite so troublesome as before. The routine of life was as comfortable as could be expected under the circumstances.

On October 25 he concluded that it was time for him to begin the more serious part of his diplomatic tasks and he wrote a letter to the Minister of Foreign Affairs in Yedo advising him that he had a letter from the President of the United States to the Emperor of Japan; that he proposed going to Yedo to deliver it, and asked that the necessary arrangements be made for his visit. As a tempting bit of diplomatic bait he threw out the suggestion that when in

Yedo he would inform the Japanese government about the intentions of Great Britain toward Japan. As he had discussed this with Sir John Bowring when he visited Hongkong, this was a matter on which he could speak not only with authority but also with the full consent and approval of the British diplomat. Only a few days before he wrote to the Minister of Foreign Affairs he had written to Secretary of State Marcy that Bowring intended to make a treaty with Japan and was prepared to use force if necessary. It would not have been contrary to the policy of Sir John to allow a hint of this to reach the Yedo officials and thereby aid Harris in concluding a treaty which would be of benefit to the British as well as to all the other powers.

Bowring was a British diplomat who was far in advance of his time in working for Anglo-American co-operation, especially in the Far East where, though the two nations were rivals in trade, they shared a common interest in breaking down the Asiatic policy of seclusion. One reason why he boldly co-operated with Americans may have been the fact that his own position was so secure and his reputation so distinguished that he did not have to consider his personal fame or credit; he could devote his energies to advancing the interests of his country, and any treaty between an Oriental and Occidental nation furthered that end.

about the surveys of the coast of Japan which the American navy had already undertaken and which, they heard, the British also had in view. They said the responsibility for these surveys had been put on their shoulders, that to prevent them was a matter of life and death, that if the surveys went on they would all have to commit hara-kiri. With what had the appearance of childish simplicity and trust they appealed to Harris to order off any surveying vessels that might approach the shores of the country. Harris explained that this was beyond his powers and then tried to make clear the peaceful and useful objectives of coastal surveys.

I then informed them that the United States Government and all the other governments of the world expended large sums in surveying their coasts and harbours, and that those surveys were published with charts so that any nation in the world could have them; that the whole world was surveyed except Japan; that these surveys made many books, and that all shipmasters purchased these books (for they were sold freely to all) before they went on any voyage to any part of the world that was new to them; that all this was done for the security of ships, it being the great object of all civilized nations to encourage commerce, which next to agriculture was the great spring of prosperity of nations; that, for the same reason, both America and England (as well as other nations) had hundreds of lighthouses on their coasts, and the channels leading into their harbours were carefully marked out with buoys, etc., etc.

This was the journal summary of a conference which continued for four hours. The officials came in apparent fear that these surveys meant preparation for an imminent attack on Japan by the combined British and American fleets. Only a week before this the naval forces of the two countries had combined in an attack on the forts of Canton; and although it is improbable that news of this event had reached Japan, the officials at Yedo may have heard rumors of the preparations.

Harris appears to have been able to convince them that their fears were groundless. When his explanations were ended Moriyama, on his knees, said he had been so worried about the matter that he had not eaten for fifty days. This may have been, and probably was, a figure of speech, although the hearty way in which all of them attacked the American-style meal and the drinks which Harris set out in their honor indicated that all had been fasting. They were undoubtedly both hungry and thirsty. They ate immense quantities of food and went through the whole list of drinks; punch, brandy, whisky, cherry bounce, champagne and cordials, but paid particular attention to the punch and champagne. It was a successful party, marred only by the fact that the host remained completely sober.

It is possible the officials were not as reassured about the innocent purpose of the survey ships as they pretended to be. Perhaps they were not even worried about the surveys but had used this as a pretext to pay a call and put their relations with Harris on a more friendly footing. Moriyama may have been indulging in a bit of play-acting when he threw himself on his knees and thanked Harris for all that he had done. But there was no doubt of their belief in Harris' sincerity and this party did mark a turning-point in the Consul-General's relations with the Japanese. Many other turning-points followed, but though all were in a favorable direction the point was never reached where frankness and honesty were met with frankness and honesty; the friendship of the American continued to be re-

142

Shimoda from the graveyard where members of Perry's fleet were buried

Mixed bathing in public bath house at Shimoda

garded as something the Japanese could turn to their advantage.

Following this interview, the Japanese officials treated Harris with a marked difference. They sent him for the first time some real venison and a real wild boar instead of the strange and unsatisfactory substitutes which had previously been palmed off on him. They added to his collection of animals a pair of very fine Japanese poodles and in contrast with their former treatment his table was now supplied with all the fruits of the season. In fact, instead of trying to starve him out the Japanese now brought him the choicest food they could find including a magnificent specimen of a golden pheasant. They noticed that he picked up sea shells and other natural curiosities and they began bringing him odd things which they thought might interest him. He had heard that there was a marsupial fish in the Bay of Yedo; the Governor gave orders to the fishermen that they should look out for specimens and bring them to Harris. None was ever found. The story of a fish which carried its young in a pocket, like a kangaroo, was probably only another of the many strange sailors' tales which had been told about Japan.

Having put their relations on a more friendly and informal basis, the Japanese immediately began to take advantage by making verbal replies to Harris' letters and pretending to be hurt when he insisted on written replies. None of the outstanding problems were solved nor did they appear to be any nearer solution than before. The only difference was that Harris had less difficulty about getting local supplies and there were obvious attempts to gain his good will.

The currency question was still unsettled but the visit

143

of ships from the Russian navy in December did enable him to strengthen his position in the controversy. The Russians too encountered difficulty over the arbitrary Japanese exchange rates, and Harris got them to agree to joint action. On their departure they had the pilotage fees and some other accounts to settle through the Japanese officials; Harris got the Russian commander to refuse to pay except on the basis for which he had been contending, that is three silver *ichibus* for one silver dollar. It was agreed between them that if the Japanese refused this basis of settlement, the difference would be placed in the hands of Harris until the arrival of a Russian Consul. Harris was greatly pleased with this arrangement which strengthened his hands—gave him, in fact, the first support or encouragement of any sort he had received since arriving in Japan. The Japanese insisted on payment of their rate, so the Russians paid one-third of the amount and left the other two-thirds with Harris for eventual adjustment as he had suggested.

Harris had written to the Minister of Foreign Affairs on October 25 advising him of the letter from the President to the Emperor and of his intention to deliver it in person at Yedo. It was not until January 7 that a reply was offered. When he called on the Governors on that date they informed him that they had been directed to give an answer to the letter. Without allowing them an opportunity to go farther, Harris inquired whether or not it was a written answer. When they admitted that it was not, he told them he could not accept a verbal reply through a third party to letters he had written. The Japanese reply was the same he had heard many times before, that it was against the law to write letters to foreigners. Harris never learned what the Governor wanted to tell him but he did take advantage of the opportunity to show them that their growing personal friendship had not blunted the edge of his resolution.

He was probably not in his usual good humor that day. He had eaten a great deal too much at the round of dinners occasioned by the visit of the Russians and was suffering from his ancient enemy, indigestion. The new year had started wrong. When out walking, Heusken had been threatened by a Japanese swordsman. In spite of many promises to remove them, the guards were still stationed in his yard. He had received no reply to his letters on the exchange question. He had invited Japanese officials to his home on New Year's day but they had declined with flimsy excuses and he had passed a lonely day without a single caller. The shopkeepers in Shimoda had refused to sell his butler some cakes. These great and petty annoyances, combined with the indigestion, doubtless added vigor to his protests; there was a four-hour interview which was recorded in some detail in his journal. When told that the laws of Japan forbade the writing of letters to foreigners:

I told them I knew better; that letters had been written by the highest officials, and even by the Emperor* himself to Commodore Perry, to the Russians and to the Dutch; that to assert such palpable falsehoods was to treat me like a child; and that, if they repeated it, I should feel myself insulted.

I then repeated what I had told the Vice-Governor about the guards and the shops and enlarged upon it, telling them it was not only a breach of the treaty, but a violation of the laws of

* In order to avoid confusion on the part of the reader it may be advisable to mention at this point that neither Perry, Harris nor any other foreigner understood that the functions of the emperor had been usurped by the shogun, who wrote the letter to Perry here referred to.

nations, and that my Government would never submit to such treatment. The Governors were in great trouble. They gave me their word of honor that the complaints about the shop-keepers should be attended to instantly, and begged me to wait until they could write to Yedo about the officers which are stationed at my house; that I mistook their nature; that they were there simply to protect me against intrusion from the Japanese; that the Shimoda people were very rude, and would be sure to give me cause of offense if the officers were not there to keep them away; and closed by saying they had no power to remove the officers, but must refer to Yedo.

In reply I told them they could not disguise the fact of my being under guard by a mere change of name; that I had no fear of the Shimoda people, who I knew were friendly when not under the eyes of their officials; that I would not consent to the delay of one day longer as to the guard; that more than three months had elapsed since I had requested their removal; and finally, so long as they remained, I declared I should consider myself a prisoner and would not leave the compound, and that I would write to my Government the manner in which they had treated me.

The trouble of the Governors increased. Finally they told me the officers should be removed.

"When?" I said.

"Very soon," was the reply.

"How many days?"

They hesitated. I repeated firmly that now that I had so strongly brought the matter up and as they had consented to the removal of the guards, every day they remained was a new outrage, and they must abide the consequences. They then said that the officers should be removed tomorrow.

Knowing their duplicity I told them the removal must be real and not nominal; that they must not post them near, or even in sight of my house; that if they made any such attempt,

I should consider it as an exaggeration of the wrong already done me. They assented to the justice of my remarks and said the officers should be brought back to the Town Hall.

They then said they hoped I would not let what had passed interrupt the good feelings heretofore existing between us; that they were most anxious to give me every proof of their friendship, etc., etc.

I told them they had a queer way of showing their friendship and hospitality; that I had been in the country four months and a half, and had never yet been invited to enter the house of a Japanese and that they had even refused to dine with me on my New Year's Day, making a flimsy excuse; that in my country New Year's Day was kept as in Japan, by making friendly visits, etc., but not a single Japanese came near me on that day, and closed by saying that in America such conduct would be called inhospitable.

I then asked if the man that threatened Mr. Heusken had been arrested. They said they did not know who it was, therefore could not arrest him. I told them the person was one of a small class; that he had a crest on his clothes and wore a sword; and that, if they did not arrest him, I should have a right to think the person was acting under direct orders from them, or according to their secret wishes, adding that hereafter, we should go out armed and any insult would be promptly punished by us, since they were either unable or unwilling to punish such persons.

I then remarked that with such a system of espionage as they had, I well knew that everything that occurred to us in our walks was reported to them.

I then enquired about the currency question and received the old reply, "waiting for a decision from Yedo." I told them that it had the appearance of a determination on their part to postpone the question indefinitely. They eagerly assured me that it was their wish to close the matter as speedily as possible.

147

So, after four hours of stormy debate, I went home, where I was agreeably surprised to find the officers and guard packing up to leave in the evening. So much for showing them a bold face.

In a brief entry of his journal on the following day Harris said: "I am determined to take firm ground with the Japanese. I will cordially meet any real offers of amity but words will not do. They are the greatest liars on earth."

## CHAPTER XIV

## A FIVE-FOOT LETTER FROM YEDO

FOR three days there was no entry in the journal and then on January 15: ¹⁸⁵⁹

Ill, ill, ill. I have cured the "Saint Anthony's Fire," but am constantly wasting away in flesh. I have a relax that takes me every four or five days, and continues about the same. I am most careful in my diet, but all is of no avail. I use exercise now in my compound, walking from five to six miles every day. My liver acts well and what it is ails me I cannot say. I left Penang on the 2nd of April last, and I am now forty pounds lighter than I was there.

At another time in referring to his constant attacks of illness and his loss in weight he makes the jocular remark that there is only enough of him left for a Vice-Consul. However, his constantly recurring illness never appears to have interfered either with his hearty appetite or his more than housewifely interest in food, for in the very next paragraph he records: "We are well supplied with wild boars' hams, some venison, plenty of fine golden pheasants, and large and good hares."

From the frequent references to food—most of it game—one is tempted to the conclusion that Harris ate a great deal too much—and that his diet of meat was not relieved by fresh vegetables. At that time Japanese were not acquainted with the common American vegetables and those

149

which they grew did not fit into the American cookbook. In fact the only vegetable grown in Japan with which Harris was familiar was the humble sweet potato.

It was not until February 24 that the Governors of Shimoda decided to break another of their supposedly inflexible laws and entertain Harris at their homes. Apparently no one had thought of applying this law to interpreter Heusken for he, with more time on his hands for visiting and with the ability to carry on a conversation in Dutch, had already made friends among some of the better-class residents of Shimoda and was a frequent visitor at their homes. Nothing had been concealed from him and he had shocked Harris by his descriptions of mixed bathing scenes in which young men and young girls sat together naked in the family bathtubs, and by his tales of the morbid sexual curiosity of the Japanese men.

One of Heusken's Japanese acquaintances wanted to learn English. When the lessons began, Heusken found that his pupil was interested only in the short four-letter words and in the English names for intimate parts of the body. The lesson was not given in private for all the women of the household crowded around. Bachelor Harris had staid old-fashioned notions about such matters. He asked the Vice-Governor if it didn't sometimes happen that a man found his bride was not a virgin. The Vice-Governor smiled reminiscently and said that as a matter of fact that had happened to him.

The entertainment provided for Harris on his first introduction to a Japanese home was especially elaborate and showed that his hosts had gone to a great deal of trouble and expense. Chairs and tables of foreign style had been acquired so that he could sit in comfort instead of having to squat in Japanese fashion on the floor. The hosts even sacrificed their own comfort to assure his—they too sat uneasily on the chairs.

While the furniture was foreign, the meal was served in Japanese style and consisted of about a dozen fish courses cooked in a wide variety of ways. In spite of his chronic indigestion and the cholera morbus from which he had suffered only a few days before, Harris appears to have done full justice to the meal. He mentions appreciatively the lobster paté, raw fish, sweet potatoes and radishes. The table was decorated with the art peculiar to the Japanese and at the end of the meal the Governor made the tea with his own hands, then presented Harris with the elaborate tea-making equipment—a genuine token of esteem and friendship. It was a beautiful party, characterized by all the refinements of which the Japanese are masters.

But as soon as the teacups were put away the conversation took the turn with which every man who has ever lived in Japan is nauseatingly familiar.

The lubricity of these people passes belief. The moment business is over, the one and only subject on which they dare converse comes up. I was asked a hundred different questions about American females, as whether single women dressed differently from the married ones, etc., etc., but I will not soil my paper with the greater part of them; but I clearly perceived that there are particulars that enter into Japanese marriage contracts that are disgusting beyond belief. Bingo-no-Kami (the second governor) informed me that one of the vice-governors was specially charged with the duty of supplying me with female society, and said if I fancied any woman, the vice-governor would procure her for me, etc., etc.

I was asked if their people could receive some instructions in

151

beating the drum when the next man-of-war came. I replied I had no doubt the commander would be willing to gratify them on that point. They said they had brass drums copied from the Dutch. They asked me about the various signals given by the beat of drums which I answered as well as I could. Then, oh, shame! They asked me if *we* had not a beat of the drum as a signal to the soldiers to go to the houses of ill-fame, and I emphatically replied "no." They evidently did not believe me, for they said, "We know the Dutch do so at Nagasaki; and all your armies are much the same." I gladly took my leave at 3 P.M. and reached home quite jaded out.

The currency question was brought up again the day following this party. Harris had been insistent on a settlement of this question only a few days after his arrival but the Shimoda officials always evaded the issue and when pressed too hard for a reply fell back on the old excuse that they were awaiting instructions from Yedo. At this time several of the Shimoda officials had just returned from the capital where Harris knew the matter must have been discussed and he pressed again for an answer. In the meantime he had formulated a definite demand, which was that American coins be exchanged for Japanese coins on a basis of weight, the American coins to be discounted 5 per cent to cover the cost of recoinage. There was a two-hour talk on this subject.

The substance of it was that they admitted the justice of my demand in part, but said my offer (five per cent) to pay for recoinage was not sufficient; that they should lose by it, and they therefore begged me to reconsider it and make them an increased offer. I asked them what was the cost of coining money in Japan. They gravely replied twenty five per cent!!! Twenty five per cent! I told them it was simply impossible;

152

that the cost in Europe and America for such labor was not one per cent; that I would bring competent moneyers from the United States who would do the whole work for five per cent and even less. They said the laws of Japan forbade the employment of foreigners about their coinage.

I endeavored to elicit a direct offer from them, but without success. Among other statements made by them was this: that gold and silver before coinage had no value, that it was the mint stamp that gave it its value, etc., etc. I told them their government had an undoubted right to deal with the precious metals produced in Japan as they pleased, but they had no such right over a foreigner, and that to attempt to exercise such a right over him would in effect be a confiscation of his property; that they might stamp pieces of paper or leather, and compel their own subjects to take them in lieu of gold and silver, but they could not expect the foreigner to take them in exchange for his merchandise, or to have his coins measured by such worthless tokens. This ground was traveled over and over again, the Japanese reasoning in a circle and trying to carry their point by simple pertinacity.

On the day this subject of currency was discussed a box was brought in with great ceremony and placed before Harris with an elaborate show of reverence. When it was opened it was found to contain five pieces of what he described to be "very poor satin damask": presents from the five members of the regency at Yedo, one piece from each.

With this introduction, a second box was brought in with an even greater show of reverence and ceremony. The Governors explained with tremendous satisfaction that it contained the answer to his two letters to Yedo in which he had told of his mission to the country and of his plans to visit the capital with the letter of the President. One of these letters had been written on board the *San Jacinto* while coming into the harbor of Shimoda and the other after the friendly conference with the Governors. When, after a great show of hesitation the box was opened, it was found to contain a sheet of paper about five feet long and eighteen inches wide—crowded with large Chinese characters and bearing the seals of the five regents. Accompanying it was a Dutch translation of the text written on a very much smaller piece of paper.

Harris did not have the letter translated until he reached home, then the imposing document was "found to be a simple announcement that all business was to be transacted with the Governors of Shimoda or Hakodate. There was not one word in reference to the President's letter to the Emperor of Japan, of which I told them I was the bearer."

At the meeting held the following day the Governors referred to the letter from Yedo, saying that it confirmed their full powers to deal with him and to treat on all matters mentioned in the two letters he had written. Undoubtedly the five-foot letter was a grievous disappointment to Harris for it blocked, for the moment, his plans to go to Yedo and negotiate directly with what he believed to be the fountain-head of authority. But during the night he had had plenty of time to reconsider his plans. He decided that if he was compelled to remain in Shimoda he would make the best of the situation and get what concessions he could from the Governors. At any rate he knew them and was on friendly terms with them, though not on terms of mutual confidence. So he asked for more explicit information about the nature of their powers.

Could they give me answers at once on all matters I might propose without waiting to hear from Yedo? They assured me in the most solemn manner that they could. I then asked could they make a new treaty without such reference. Their answer soon proved what I before suspected,—that, in any minor matter, they could decide, but, on any important one, they could only hear and report.

Having learned what their powers were, Harris did not discuss the matter any further but proceeded to business at once. The Governors wished to debate the currency question again but he insisted on its postponement. There were a number of propositions he had in mind to which he knew they could offer no objections and his strategy was to bring these up in rapid-fire order, and so gradually build up an approach to the discussion of questions which would be more difficult of solution.

I then stated that the port of Nagasaki had been opened to the Russians as a place where the ship could obtain necessary supplies and coals for steamers and I demanded the same rights for the Americans. This was finally agreed to. My next was, that American ships in want of supplies and not having money, that goods should be taken in payment. They said this was already agreed to by our treaty. I told them, if that was the case, of course they could have no objection to reaffirming it, and this was agreed to. My next was that Americans committing offences in Japan should be tried by the consul and punished if guilty according to Japanese laws.* To my great and agreeable surprise this was agreed to without demur.

* This reference to the laws of Japan, as it appeared in the Journal, has been referred to as a "slip of the pen" and it has been suggested that what Harris really proposed was the regulation as it later appeared in the treaty, providing that Americans be tried under American laws. What appears more probable is that he first obtained assent to the agreement of trial by Consul and later expanded this to provide for the application of American laws. The many laws of Japan to which the officials referred so glibly were not

I next told them that I demanded the right for Americans to lease ground, buy, build, repair or alter such buildings at their pleasure and that they should be supplied with materials and labor for such purposes whenever they might require it. I told them I founded this claim on the 12th and 13th articles made with the Dutch at Nagasaki, on the 9th of November, 1855, by which all the ground of Deshima was leased to the Dutch and the buildings sold to them; that they also had the right to build, alter or repair, etc., and that I claimed these same privileges under the 9th article of the Treaty of Kanagawa.*

The governors were amazed. They never heard of any such convention. It did not, could not exist. When, where and by whom was it made? . . . Now will it be believed that during all this time (more than one hour) the governors had an authentic copy of that very convention lying before them in a dispatch box? It was so, and all this barefaced falsehood was a fair specimen of Japanese diplomacy.

He had many occasions to refer to the lack of honesty of the Japanese, ranging from adroit evasions to barefaced lies, and was reluctantly led to the conclusion that they never told the truth. This was wrong for they were truthful at times but as it was often impossible for him to distinguish the true from the false, the truth was often as deceptive as the most adroit lies. In his journal a few days later he says: "There was less falsehood in their replies to this point than there was to the preceding one, but this

published and the stipulation that Americans be tried under those laws would have required that these laws be made public to foreigners. The British Treaty which Admiral Stirling had negotiated at Nagasaki, after the conclusion of the Perry Treaty, provided that sailors who broke the laws of Japan should be handed over to their officers for punishment.

* This was the usual "most favoured nation clause" and provided that any rights or privileges granted to other nations should accrue to the United States "without any consultation or delay."

arose from want of opportunity rather than want of inclination."

After some of the other questions had been settled, the currency question was brought up. The Japanese for the first time discussed it with some show of reasonableness. They agreed that it was not right to exchange the dollar for 1600 *seni* as that was the number of *seni* given in exchange for their silver coin, which was one-third the weight of the dollar. They now proposed to weigh the coins brought to Japan by Americans, weight for weight, and from the amount of Japanese coin to be paid in exchange to deduct 15 per cent to pay for what they said would be the loss of melting and coining.

With this proposal Harris had gained his most important point, which was that American coins be exchanged on a basis of weight instead of being accepted as new bullion; but the proposal to discount American coins by 15 per cent was not acceptable; he suggested 5 per cent. No headway was being made in arguing this detail when he sprang a surprise by saying he had something of great importance to communicate to them confidentially. When the room was cleared of all but the Governors:

I read to them an extract from a letter to me from the Secretary of State, which was to the effect that, if the Japanese sought to evade the treaty, the President would not hesitate to ask Congress to give him power to use such arguments as they could not resist. The fluttering was fearful—the effect strong. They thanked me for the confidence I had placed in them by reading that part of the Secretary's letter, and asked if they might communicate the same to their government.

This extract was from the instructions Secretary of State Marcy had given Harris in Washington more than a year before. Harris of course granted the Governors full permission to tell the Yedo officials about it as he had read the letter with that purpose in view. But the impression made on the Governors was not so strong as he had believed. When the conferences were resumed after this semblance of a threat they did not progress any more satisfactorily than before. To a categorical demand that they give an answer on the currency and other questions, the Governors were still evasive and dilatory. They asked him to put all his propositions in writing. This he refused to do on the ground that "once I had placed my name to a paper, it could not be modified—and I wished to leave a door open by which we might arrive at a solution of the question."

Harris by this time was beginning to adopt the Japanese method of conducting negotiations—to refuse every request whether reasonable or unreasonable or to grant it only in some modified form or as a return for some concession. This matter of the written demands was finally settled by an arrangement that Heusken should, as if on his own responsibility, give them an unsigned memorandum, setting forth all the things which Harris had asked for.

The real reason for all these delays and evasions was the fact that the Governors did not dare to exercise the limited powers which had been given them, were afraid to accept any responsibility or come to any decisions without referring the larger controversial points to Yedo. Apparently the communication from the Secretary of State was not sufficient to stir the Shimoda Governors but did stir the Yedo officials to an activity which was most unusual for them. Only a few days after it had been for-

Delivery at Yokohama of the presents brought by Commodore Perry

Teahouse and garden in Yedo.

warded to Yedo and a reply received the Governors were more reasonable in the matter of the currency question. They now offered to accept American coins at a discount of only 6 per cent as compared to the 15 per cent they had formerly offered and the 5 per cent which Harris had demanded. This meant that whereas the dollar had formerly been exchanged for only 1600 *seni*, it would, under this new arrangement, exchange for 4760 *seni*. But Harris was now in no mind for compromise and refused to budge from his figure of 5 per cent. On the other hand the Governors must have had very positive instructions in the matter for they also refused to alter their position.

The Governor, the Prince of Shinano, rose from his seat and came to me; and, while standing, begged me as a personal favor to him to yield the one per cent of difference; that they were most anxious to have the matter settled, but that it was impossible for them to go any farther than they had done, and (mark this) that, if they took the coin of the Americans at less than six per cent, the government would lose by the operation of recoinage. Contrast this with their solemn assurance that it cost twenty-five per cent to coin the money of Japan. The mendacity of these men passes all human belief. We finally adjourned to some day next week. I am really ill, yet I am forced day after day to listen to useless debates, or points that have been exhausted, and are only varied by some new falsehood.

## CHAPTER XV

# THE CONVENTION OF SHIMODA

O**N MARCH** 9, 1857, Harris' loneliness was relieved by the arrival of the *Messenger Bird* which had sailed for Japan from San Francisco by way of Honolulu. This was the second American sailing-ship he had seen since the *San Jacinto* sailed away so abruptly. The *General Pierce* had called on a speculative trading venture but sailed away again when the Japanese refused to purchase the damaged cargo of ammunition she carried. The brief stay had not provided a pleasant interlude for the exile of Shimoda. Two gunboats of the Russian navy were the most recent visitors, in November. Harris and the Russians had got along splendidly together. When Harris went on board the Russian corvette for dinner he was given a salute of thirteen guns in spite of the fact that according to Russian regulations he was entitled to only eleven guns. The Russian commander explained that he did this because he had given the Governor of Shimoda a similar salute and did not want it to appear that he considered Harris of lower rank. Harris offered the services of his Chinese washman to launder the soiled linen of the Russian commander; the latter sent his men to repair the American flagstaff. There were many friendly dinner parties and Harris ate so much rich Russian food that it was some weeks before he recovered his usual state of semi-ill-health.

The call of the *Messenger Bird* was especially welcome. Mr. Hall, the 18-year-old super-cargo, brought him some newspapers of such a recent date as November 8. These were four months old, but until then the most recent American newspaper he had seen since arriving in Japan was more than ten months old. From the papers Mr. Hall brought he learned that Buchanan had been elected President. He had in fact been inaugurated the day after Harris made the threatening announcement to the Governors in which he quoted a letter from Secretary Marcy. He had anticipated the election of Buchanan but it was a relief to know that it was an accomplished fact, for it meant that with the Democrats still in power he would be allowed to continue and possibly bring to completion the work he had barely started. Secretary Marcy's political slogan, "to the victors belong the spoils," was an expression of policy which other parties derided but did not denounce. There can be no doubt but that in the event of a wholly unexpected victory of Fremont over Buchanan every Democratic appointee would have been swept out of office.

The visit of the *Messenger Bird* was more than a welcome relief from the monotony of isolation. As Mr. Hall had ship supplies to purchase his visit came at an opportune time: it gave Harris a sound reason to press for a final settlement of the currency question. This had in fact been settled to the extent that the young super-cargo's bills were payable on the basis of one American dollar being equal in value to three Japanese *ichibus*, less a discount of 6 per cent. The Governors had refused to budge from this position though Harris continued to insist that 5 per cent discount was adequate. In the end the pertinacity of the Governors prevailed. It was finally arranged that

Mr. Hall would settle accounts on the 6 per cent basis but that this would not be taken as a precedent.

The *Messenger Bird* was the first American ship to benefit by the more favorable rate of exchange and that provided the only bright spot in this first American attempt to sell goods to the Japanese. Mr. Hall did not in fact succeed in selling anything because his prices were too high, but he did purchase a quantity of Japanese products for sale elsewhere. Under the old exchange rate his bill would have been more than $3,300 but under the new rate he settled for about one-third of that amount, a saving of more than $2,000.

Harris took a great deal of satisfaction in this but a few days later when he came to settle with the youthful but crafty Mr. Hall he found that his own countrymen were just as resourceful as the Japanese when it came to juggling with exchange. The supplies which Harris had bought in New York and supplemented in Hongkong were almost exhausted, and he bought some provisions from Mr. Hall in spite of his outrageously high prices. He paid for these in silver coin as was customary; but when Mr. Hall settled for his consular fees he wanted to pay in gold coin, which would have meant a loss to Harris of about 75 per cent. In Japan the ratio of gold to silver was a little more than three to one, instead of sixteen to one. In his journal Harris commented: "It takes a New England man to do such things."

Relations with the Governors continued on an increasingly friendly basis. The day the two young Japanese servants moved into his household, Harris began to increase his knowledge of the language by learning the Japanese names of familiar objects. Only a few weeks later he was able to give all directions to the servants in their own tongue. By April 14 his studies of the language had progressed so satisfactorily that he secured a copy of a Japanese dictionary and the officials promised to bring him some schoolbooks, novels and works on history.

By an arrangement forced on him regarding provisions for his household, he would requisition what he wanted and the officials would send the supplies to him. The understanding was that he would be charged the current market prices, but in practice he was overcharged for everything and only by constant complaints was able to reduce prices to anything like a reasonable basis. When he had asked for two Japanese boys as servants the Vice-Governor had calmly assured him that the usual wage for servants of this sort was $16 per month, which was, of course, a great deal more than the average skilled artisan would earn. After four months of haggling over the matter the wage was finally settled at $2 per month. In fact his expenses for Japanese servants provided less financial worry than anything else on his simple budget. He now had five and their total cost was $132 per annum, out of which they provided for their own food. On the other hand the four Chinese servants cost him more than $700 per annum in addition to their board.

When at the end of seven months the officials brought him a statement of account he found that he owed no less than 2.087,009 *seni*, but put into terms of American currency this amounted to only $447. He went very carefully into the matter of expenses and finally came to the very satisfying conclusion that he could live on $2,000 a year, which would enable him to save $3,000 a year from his salary. For several days the pages of his journal were full of scattered references to this important matter which was worked out in the casual manner of the average housewife, with frequent changes in the total as he thought of things he had forgotten to include.

There was, for example, the matter of rent which he had forgotten to provide for in his original calculation. So long as he occupied the temple set apart for his use there was no rent to pay, but when a house was specially built for his occupancy, as had been promised, he would undoubtedly have to pay rent for it. He had also forgotten to take into consideration the fact that he was charging Heusken a dollar a day for his board, also that the horse and his palanquin—which he had bought—would not have to be replaced for some time and so would not constitute a recurrent expense. In the end he came to the conclusion that his expenses would be $1,750, leaving him with a good margin over the original figure of $3,000; then he thought of something else he had forgotten and returned to his original figure of $2,000. He had from the first been very insistent on the building of a house for his occupancy but now he said no more about it.

Perhaps this reflection that he would have to pay rent for a house built for him caused him to change his mind, or perhaps after months of work he had managed to get comfortably settled in the temple, had become attached to it and did not want to leave. He had, in spite of many obstacles, managed to surround himself with homely comforts. A small plot of adjoining land was rented as a garden, and there was an increasing number of occupants in his pig-pen and hen-house. The pigeons which the cat had killed were replaced by others which were more carefully guarded. In his living-room there was an interesting collection of caged birds whose care helped to relieve his loneliness. None of these things had been acquired without a struggle, for exhibitions of Japanese friendship and hospitality alternated with displays of petty and absurd churlishness. When he started to plant his little garden the Japanese officials brought him twenty grains of corn and seven watermelon seeds, which they said was all they could procure. They explained that he was late in starting his garden and all their seeds had been planted!

After receiving his bill from the officials for the seven months' supplies Harris waited more than a month to settle, holding out for a discount of only 5 per cent on his American coins while the Japanese insisted on 6 per cent. Each side was obdurate and the controversy finally resulted in a typically Oriental compromise. The Japanese accepted payment of the account with American dollars discounted at 5 per cent, with the understanding that the next settlement would be at a discount of 6 per cent, the following at 5 per cent and so on, alternately, until a final agreement was reached. He did not settle for his household expenses until June 6. His bill by this time amounted to the alarming total of 3,476,594 *seni*, but the whole was settled for $699. He pointed out that if the accounts had been paid on the basis admitted by Commodore Perry it would have amounted to $2,173.

As day after day, then week after week went by following the departure of the *Messenger Bird*, with no calls of American ships and no mail or news from home, the comforts of his bachelor's mess palled on him and the journal was full of entries which reflected his loneliness and despondency.

On April 18 he wrote, "My last letters from the United

States were dated March 18, 1856. More than 13 months ago." At that time Harris was in Penang anxiously awaiting the arrival of the *San Jacinto*. The letters he referred to were the ones he had received in June on his arrival in Hongkong after negotiating the treaty with Siam. Now he was awaiting the arrival of the *San Jacinto* even more anxiously than before, for he was very ill and wanted to see Dr. Wood.

"My last letters from the Department of State were dated in October 1855, more than eighteen months ago," he wrote on April 25. "It is too long a period to leave me here alone, and some order should be given to ensure more frequent communication with me."

The fact that a man-of-war was soon due had been impressed on the Governors and as they continued to dally Harris became more and more convinced that he would get no action until a man-of-war did arrive. In his pessimistic journal entry of April 25 he wrote: "If I had a vessel of war here, I should have speedy answers to my demands but I feel sure they will not be settled so long as no ship-of-war comes here."

Nevertheless he went ahead with the details of the negotiations and on the following day set down a summary of points on which a definite agreement had been reached though nothing had been agreed to in writing.

I feel sure that what I have accomplished will give satisfaction. I have settled the currency so that one dollar goes as far almost as three did when Perry left the question. I have opened the port of Nagasaki to American ships wanting supplies. Americans are only to be amenable to American authority for offenses committed in Japan. American ships in distress and who have no money can pay for all necessary supplies by barter.

166

I have fought the battles, and, although *I* may not receive the victory, yet victory will come and be owing to my labors.

The easy way in which the Japanese had agreed to giving extra-territorial rights to the Americans had constituted the one pleasant surprise in the negotiations. If they had put up any arguments against the provision that Americans be subject only to American laws and be tried by their own officials, it is improbable that Harris would have held out very strongly on this point, for neither he nor Secretary Marcy was in favor of it. Secretary Marcy had instructed him to include the clause in the treaty but only because he feared the Senate would not ratify a treaty which did not contain it. As for the Japanese, they probably did not give the matter very serious consideration. At the time the only Americans likely to commit offenses were the men from sailing-ships, and the Japanese would be relieved of possibly unpleasant responsibilities if these men could be turned over to the American authorities for punishment. That was the attitude which had been taken by the Chinese authorities and in neither country was there any realization of the serious implications involved by this surrender of their sovereignty.

As day after day passed with no ship calling and no news from home Harris became more and more despondent in spite of the favorable progress he was making with the negotiations. On May 5, 1857, he wrote:

It is now eight months and three days since the *San Jacinto* left here. Commodore Armstrong promised me he would be here again in six months. I am a prey to unceasing anxiety. I have not heard from Washington since I left the United States, say October 1855.

What can be the cause of this prolonged absence of an American man-of-war? Where are the English? Where are the French? And, above all, where is the Russian Consul? He should have been here before this. I am only nine days distant from Hongkong, yet I am more isolated than any American official in any part of the world.

I have important intelligence to send to my government—intelligence that will give an immediate spur to our trade with Japan; yet here it remains, month after month, without my being able to communicate it to my Government, or enabling my countrymen to benefit by it. The absence of a man-of-war also tends to weaken my influence with the Japanese. They have yielded nothing except from *fear*, and any future ameliorations of our intercourse will only take place after a demonstration of force on our part.

I will not suppose this apparent neglect arises from indifference or idleness on the part of our naval commanders out here. I, therefore, am left a prey to all sorts of imaginations as to the detaining causes.

A few days later he had a small belvedere erected on a nearby hill overlooking the bay and there during the hot summer months he spent his idle hours enjoying the cool breezes and looking out to sea for the first glimpse of an American flag.

During this period, when he was so seriously ill, he allowed nothing to interfere with his work—not even the tortures of cholera morbus—but kept his journal with even more than the usual meticulous care, setting down daily the details of every interview with Japanese officials. It is quite obvious that he was living in fear of death and that his journal and all of his papers were kept up to date, in perfect order, so that if one of his frequent attacks of cholera morbus should prove fatal, his successor could carry on the work with the least possible delay. Some of the entries in his journal suggest the phraseology of a last will and testament. After a very severe gastric attack he took the precaution of appointing Heusken as Vice-Consul.

Days of despondency caused by illness and loneliness were followed by days of elation when he was able to record some actual progress in the convention he was negotiating with the Governors. In a moment of despondency he had been sure that he could accomplish nothing without the presence of a man-of-war but on June 8 he was able to write in his journal:

I have at last carried every point triumphantly with the Japanese, and have got everything conceded that I have been negotiating for since last September. Among my papers will be found a copy of the convention which contains the following provisions:

1st. Opens the port of Nagasaki to American ships.

2nd. Gives the right of permanent residence to Americans at Shimoda and Hiakodate and the right to appoint a Vice-Consul at the latter port.

3rd. Settles the currency, so that where we paid $100 we may now pay only $34.50.*

4th. Americans to be exclusively under the control of their Consuls and to be tried by American law.

5th. Concedes the right of the Consul-General to go where he pleases in Japan, and to be furnished with Japanese money to enable him in person, or by his servants, to make his purchases without the intervention of any Japanese official. This is even more than I was instructed to ask for in my special instructions dated October 4, 1855. No class of Americans is

* In this long debated matter of the coinage discount Harris was unable to get the Japanese to agree to his contention and the Shimoda convention provides for a discount of 6 per cent.

named in the second article, so that missionaries may actually come and reside in Japan.

⁜This convention, which was signed nine days later, was by all counts a great diplomatic victory and was due entirely to his own patience and persistence and the fact that he had partially allayed the suspicions of the Japanese, convinced them that instead of being a sharp and grasping bargainer he was asking only for what he believed to be fair and to the interests of Japan as well as of his own country. The man-of-war he hoped for and had actually threatened had not arrived. Even if the British or French had begun to negotiate for a treaty, as they were expected to do, or if the Russian Consul had come to Shimoda, his task would have been easier. But his long and discouraging labors, his constant fight against illness, and especially the neglect of the State Department, robbed him of all the joy of accomplishment. After setting down this successful achievement he wrote:

Am I elated by this success? Not a whit. I know my dear countrymen but too well to expect any praise for what I have done, and I shall esteem myself lucky if I am not removed from office, not for what I have done, but because I have not made a commercial treaty that would open Japan as freely as England is open to us.

Besides, it is so easy to criticize and so agreeable to condemn. It is much more pleasant to write imbecile, ass or fool, than to say able, discreet and competent.

Poor lonely old bachelor! The Japanese lied to him and met frankness with evasion. His servants stole. His secretary let the fire go out. He was out of provisions and short of money. The Secretary of State did not write to him. He suffered from indigestion and was losing weight rapidly. And on top of all that his pet canary refused to hatch out the eggs she had laid. He was fighting so persistently against disease that during May he walked an average of more than ten miles a day. He was desperately in need of a doctor. He loved good food and in spite of his illness had a hearty appetite. Yet he dare not eat anything but rice and chicken. In fact he had little else. At the time the very successful convention was signed he had been out of flour, bread, butter, lard, hams, bacon—in fact out of every kind of foreign food supply—for more than two months and had been reduced to what was practically a Japanese diet. He had given up tobacco entirely. He liked good company but here he was as if on a desert island. A desert island would probably have been preferable, for here he was worse than isolated. He was surrounded by people who met his friendly advances with distinct suspicion, who constantly wounded and offended him by their atrocious lies. The government which he was serving so faithfully had apparently forgotten him entirely. He had negotiated the treaty with Siam more than a year ago but there had not been one word from Washington about it.

No wonder he found little joy in his lonely victory.

## CHAPTER XVI

# THE VAIN WAIT FOR THE *SAN JACINTO*

W ITH the Shimoda convention signed Harris was able
to turn his undivided attention to the task which
was uppermost in his mind—the delivery of President
Pierce's letter to the ruler at Yedo. This letter was addressed to "His Majesty the Emperor of Japan" with the
chummy salutation: "Great and Good Friend," and Harris
presumed that the Emperor and the powerful but mysterious person who was referred to as the "Ziogoon" were
one and the same person. Perry had thought the same
thing; he did not live to learn that the many presents he
had brought for the Emperor of Japan never reached His
Majesty but rotted and rusted in one of the warehouses
of the Tokugawa family, the clan which ruled the country
in the name of the Emperor. On his arrival in Shimoda
Harris had written about the President's letter. He wrote
again to the Council of State on October 25, and instead
of asking permission to visit Yedo, boldly announced his
intention of going there, instructing that arrangements be
made for the trip. He received no direct reply to either of
these letters, but they were answered indirectly through
the Shimoda Governors who made every effort to secure
the letter themselves and prevent Harris' going to Yedo.
The convention concluded with him was, in effect, a practical demonstration that a visit to the capital was not necessary, that all diplomatic business could be arranged at
Shimoda.

Although Harris had been in Japan now for almost a year, he had not learned what every Japanese knew, that the Emperor of Japan was a powerless recluse in Kyoto and that while the powerful Tokugawa family in Yedo ruled in his name, they flouted his authority; that the ruler of Japan was a *tabu*[*] concealed as carefully as the *tabu* of Polynesian witchcraft. The *tabu* was made all the more effective by the system of concealed government which extended through all gradations of authority. As Harris discovered very early in his negotiations, he was never to deal with anyone in authority, but always with a spokesman who had to refer all decisions to some one else whose identity was unknown and mysterious. Baffled and puzzled by this strange delegation of authority, Harris thought that by going to Yedo he would be able to deal directly with the rulers of the country—only to find when he finally reached there that the mystery as to who ruled the country was as deep as it had been when he was isolated at Shimoda.

The fact that the President's letter was addressed to the Emperor, that in fact all foreign governments named him as the ruler of the country, threw terror into the hearts of the Tokugawa usurpers who were able to retain their supreme power only by keeping the other powerful and jealous families of the country in subjection. During the centuries that the Emperor had been kept a figurehead there had been many plots on the part of other families to overthrow the Tokugawas under the pretext of restoring the Emperor to his ancient power. This would have meant, in effect, that the power now exercised by the Tokugawas would be transferred to another usurper and their power legalized by imperial sanction, just as that of the Tokugawas had been. It was by following this procedure that the Tokugawas had become the absolute rulers of the coun-

* *Golden Bough*, by J. G. Frazer.

try; and the head of their family, who was known as the Shogun, had in the minds of all foreigners come to be confused with the Emperor himself.

Thus the question, whether Japan should be opened to the foreigner or the policy of exclusion continued, was not considered so much on the basis of its problematical benefits to the country, but—how would it affect the interests of various parties or families? And in the background of every discussion was the fear of what might happen if the foreign powers should learn that the Emperor did not live in Yedo but in Kyoto and their knowledge of that fact strengthen the growing movement against the Tokugawas. The foreign powers might attempt to negotiate with the Emperor at Kyoto.

It was because of these plots against the Tokugawa family that the peculiar system of government by hostage had been developed. While representatives of the local feudal lords remained at home (like the Governors of Shimoda) other members of the family were required to take up their residence in Yedo where they would be subject to swift and cruel punishment if their relatives in the province showed any evidences of disloyalty or of treasonable designs. Yedo was, as a matter of fact, a huge city of political prisoners, and beneath the apparently calm surface and unified front of Japan there seethed a hundred family feuds and dozens of secret plots to sap the power of the Tokugawas.

After having negotiated the Shimoda Convention without having allowed Harris to visit Yedo, the officials apparently thought he would no longer be so insistent and they could continue to enforce his prison-like existence in Shimoda. The Shimoda convention did not give the

174

Consul-General the undisputed right to free travel in Japan. It admitted his right to travel beyond the seven Japanese miles to which the Perry Treaty had restricted him, but as a price for that concession the Japanese exacted a promise that he would not take advantage of it except in case of emergency such as a shipwreck. With these preparations completed the Governors attempted a final settlement of the question of the delivery of the letter. Only a few days after the convention was signed they showed Harris what purported to be an imperial mandate under the signature and seal of the Emperor commanding them to receive the President's letter and bring it to Yedo. They appeared to be quite dumbfounded when he refused to yield to this mandate. The Prince of Shinano even hinted that he might be compelled to commit hara-kiri if Harris persisted in his refusal to hand over the letter.

The Governor knew that he would be severely blamed by the Yedo officials for failure to comply with the mandate and he waited for two weeks before he set out for Yedo to report that Harris, in spite of the mandate, refused to deliver the letter to anyone but the Emperor. In the meantime the Japanese bombarded Harris with new arguments. They assured him that it was quite preposterous ever to think of an audience with the Emperor "as the laws of Japan forbid it." Harris was no longer impressed by these citations regarding the laws of Japan with which the officials tried to settle almost every issue. They had told him only a few months before this that the laws of Japan did not allow an official to visit a foreigner, that the State Council could not write to foreigners, and both of these laws had been broken. It was obvious that these so-called laws were extremely pliable.

The signing of the Shimoda convention was a genuine accomplishment, but all further progress appeared to be blocked. Harris was not even able to inform his government that the convention had been signed, for the man-of-war he had been expecting so long had not arrived. When July 4 came he recorded the fact that he had never before felt more miserable and wretched, but nevertheless he carried out the routine of the day's celebration. He arranged with the Japanese to fire a national salute of twenty guns in honor of the day and was not made any happier by the fact that they sent him a bill for the powder. They must have charged the guns very lightly, for the bill was less than two dollars. This stingy salute was fired on a Saturday. The following Monday he gave up all hope of seeing Commodore Armstrong of the *San Jacinto* and began making plans to send some letters overland to Hakodate where they might be picked up by an American whaling vessel. The distance from Shimoda to Hakodate was less than 600 miles, yet the postal arrangements were so primitive that it required 35 days to transmit a letter. He was sure the Japanese would open and read the letters so he wrote very cautiously. He did not dare chance sending any important documents to the State Department.

The summer months dragged by so miserably that for the first time since his departure from New York he gave up attempts to make the usual daily entries in his journal. At first there would be a gap of a day, then of several days, then of more than a week. One of these long lapses was broken to record his bitter disappointment that a ship which had been sighted on July 23 did not come into port.

The cannon from the lookout hill was fired at noon today, and it caused such joy as only can be felt by those who have been living isolated, as I have been, for the past eleven months. Mr. Heusken ran like a deer to the top of the signal hill and came back, breathless and streaming with sweat, to say that there was a ship in sight, about ten miles to the south of the harbor; that as the wind was not very fresh she would not come in for some time. He started again for Vandalia Point (the most southern point) to watch her approach. At four p.m. he returned quite downhearted. The ship had disappeared in the blue haze a little after one o'clock and had not reappeared; she appeared to be standing northeast. We are now in doubt what it can mean, but think she must be bound here, else why approach so near.

The following morning Harris did not wait for reports from Heusken but was up at daylight and off to the east hills that command a view of the Bay of Yedo and the South Pacific. "Alas! No ship could be seen; whoever she was, it was clear she was not bound for Shimoda. I never had anything try my philosophy so hardly as this."

Following this bitter disappointment he gave his third and last revolver to one of the Governors, and except for a brief routine note about the weather there was no further entry in the journal for more than two weeks.

It was not until September 7 that the signal gun was fired again and Mr. Heusken again raced to the top of the hill. On his return he confirmed the fact that a heavy ship was standing in for the harbor. But he could not make out the flag as a steady breeze blew the colors so that they could not be seen. It was obvious that she was not the long expected *San Jacinto* but a sailing-ship. Just about dusk the wind fell off and all hopes that the ship would anchor that night were dashed. But Harris could not bear the suspense of waiting through the night. It was now more than a year since the *San Jacinto* had sailed away. The last fellow countryman he had seen had been the precocious Mr. Hall of the *Messenger Bird*. Although the visiting ship was about ten miles from shore Mr. Heusken hired a pilot boat and went out to visit her. Well past midnight he returned with the joyful news that this was the American sloop-of-war, *Portsmouth*, eighteen days out of Shanghai. He brought back a few letters and a package of newspapers and the greetings of Captain Foote who promised to call the following day. Harris did not go to bed that night but sat up reading and re-reading the letters and papers.

About noon the ship anchored and Captain Foote called. The Consul-General's usual calm and dignity deserted him. Tears of joy filled his eyes and he was visibly affected. Like others he found the vocabulary of gratitude inadequate.

But the news Captain Foote brought filled his mind with doubts about the good faith of Commodore Armstrong. At the time the *Portsmouth* sailed from Shanghai the *San Jacinto* had been there for three months, and could easily have reached Shimoda in a week. He also learned that Captain Foote was not calling at Shimoda, as Harris had supposed, on orders from Commodore Armstrong, but rather in spite of him. Captain Foote, who was enroute to the American whaling ship rendezvous at Hakodate, had at first been given strict instructions not to enter the harbor of Shimoda; when consent was finally granted on the plea of shore leave for the crew, he was told to stay the shortest possible time. Commodore Armstrong had added ungraciously that he would probably have to bring Harris away.

To increase the distress caused by this story, there was no letter from Commodore Armstrong to explain his failure to return in March as he had promised. There were friendly letters to Harris from Captain Bell and the officers of the *San Jacinto*, but not one word from the commodore. If he had set out deliberately to thwart Harris in his work, he could not have acted differently. He had done nothing he promised to do. He had not even arranged for the forwarding of the Consul-General's official mail, which was all lying in Hongkong. Perhaps the commodore forgot his promise to return in six months, as that was only a personal promise. It appears that the State Department had told Harris that the *San Jacinto* would return in three months, but Armstrong said he had no instruction to that effect. Harris was so hurt and surprised that he wrote at some length in his long-neglected journal:

It appears that Commodore Armstrong has been occupied from December to June in protecting the British Colony of Hongkong, thus enabling Admiral Seymour (British) to employ more of his force in active hostilities against the Chinese. He found himself able to send a ship to Manila to inquire about some Americans who are imprisoned there under a charge of murder, and he was also able to send another to Singapore to inquire into—what? A case of salvage!!! However, let him pass with this addition. I informed Captain Foote that all my dispatches from the government were at Hakodate where they had remained since last May, and that, as he was going there, I asked him to touch here on his return and give me my letters. It would seem as though the Commodore had foreseen this request, for he positively ordered Captain Foote on leaving

Hakodate to stretch out one hundred and fifty miles from land, while his direct route would have carried him about twenty five miles south of Shimoda.

Whatever may have been his grief and disappointment over the churlish attitude and the apparent personal animosity of Commodore Armstrong, these were soon forgotten in the joy of human contacts. He also forgot his illness, and the journal was crowded daily with lively entries about the dinners on board the *Portsmouth*—the first satisfactory meals he had enjoyed for months—and the salute of thirteen guns which he received when he came on board. The salute was "from the heavy sixty-eight pounders which were loaded with full charges and not with the usual reduced charge which is used for saluting." Like an excited small boy, he could not sleep.

Captain Foote was able to give him his first news about the Siam Treaty, for Foote's ship had brought Consul Bradley back to Bangkok after the treaty had been ratified by the Senate. Ships were already loading from New York and San Francisco for the Siam trade. This indirect news was the only word Harris had received regarding his official business since leaving New York almost two years before. Captain Foote was also the first fellow-American he could tell about the Shimoda Convention, which had been signed nearly three months previously. It is not surprising that, with boyish eagerness, he showed his visitor the important document at the first opportunity nor that he listened gratefully to praise.

Always a generous host, Harris was embarrassed that he could not return the hospitality of the *Portsmouth*, could offer his guests nothing but rice and tough chicken. He had, in fact, been out of bread since early in June, had no hams, bacon, lard or any of the usual food supplies considered as necessities. So the visitors gave him flour, lard, hominy, tea, a dozen fine Virginia hams, and some smoked tongue.

Searching through his scanty stores for presents to send officers of the *San Jacinto*, Harris found a bolt of fine Japanese silk for Commodore Armstrong.

## CHAPTER XVII

# INVITED TO COME TO YEDO

POSSIBLY the arrival of the *Portsmouth* completely drove from Harris' mind momentarily the most important thing that had happened to him since his arrival in Japan— an invitation by the State Council to visit Yedo, and to have an audience with the Ziogoon, or Shogun, to whom he would present the letter of the President addressed to the Emperor. According to a dispatch to Secretary of State Cass* which was forwarded by the *Portsmouth,* he told of the interview with the Governors at which he received the welcome news. The interview took place on September 7, the day the signal gun announced the sighting of the *Portsmouth,* but it was not until some time after the *Portsmouth* sailed that he set it down in his journal, when he fixed the date as September 22.

He had been ill when the *Portsmouth* arrived and the excitement caused by the break in his hermit-like existence was so great that he could not sleep; there were many gaps in his journal. This may explain the confusion in dates but it is significant that the decision of the Yedo officials to invite him was reached before the arrival of the *Portsmouth.* The Council of State was not spurred to action by the arrival of a man-of-war, though news of the concentration of an allied French and British fleet for an

* On the inauguration of President Buchanan, Lewis Cass succeeded W. L. Marcy as Secretary of State.

attack on North China may have been a contributing factor in bringing the Shogun's government to the point of sending for Harris. He had as frequently as opportunity offered hinted that unless Japan signed a treaty with him, which he was ready to conclude by peaceful negotiations, a treaty would be forced on the country by the armed forces of Europe. This was what England and France were now preparing to do in China—the largest and most powerful of the Asiatic countries.

The Prince of Shimoda told him that he should make the journey to the capital in the most honorable manner. After so many rebuffs and discouragements it is not to be wondered at that this entirely unexpected news aroused his suspicions. He was afraid that it would be followed by insistence on some condition or other which he could not accept and so throw on him the responsibility for failure to deliver the President's letter; the Japanese could then say that he had been invited to Yedo but had declined the invitation.

He was so thoroughly disillusioned by his experiences with Japanese officials that he was in danger of becoming completely sceptical. A dozen times he had noted what he thought to be evidence of friendship and frankness and had accepted them eagerly, without question, only to find that they were not sincere. But careful and perhaps suspicious questioning failed to reveal that there were any traps concealed in this invitation. The Governors did make a hesitant request that he prostrate himself and knock his head in Oriental fashion when face to face with the great ruler, but when Harris said that even the mention of such a thing was offensive to him, they dropped the suggestion and did not refer to it again. It was agreed that the customs at European courts be followed, that he would salute the ruler with three ceremonial bows.

The Governors did insist that on the journey from Shimoda to Yedo a fixed itinerary be followed, with stops at certain places at certain hours, a stipulation which was much more reasonable than Harris understood it to be. In spite of their assurances that he was to travel in the most honorable manner, he took no chances but

informed them that I should be willing to agree to such hours as might prove best, and to stop where I could be best accommodated, but I could not bind myself beforehand to any hour of march; that I must not only be free in my action, but that the escort attending me must be under my command, exclusively; that they would find me a reasonable man, quite ready to adopt any proper suggestions on those points on the road, but could not be bound to comply with their regulations before I knew what might occur.

In order to remove any pretext for interference on the part of the Japanese, he arranged to provide for his own food on the journey and also to pay the wages of his own guards, bearers, grooms, etc. Fortunately for the success of this arrangement he did not have to make any cash disbursements for he had no money. The funds he had brought from New York had been exhausted and he had not been able to collect any salary. He had complained bitterly about the regulations compelling him to make all his purchases and employ all his servants through the Japanese officials but now he found it very convenient to have them act as his bankers.

The Governors agreed to everything he suggested. Then they gave some hint of what had been meant by traveling in "the most honorable manner" by saying that it would probably require about two months to complete the preparations for this journey of less than a hundred miles. The Dutch for many years had made annual pilgrimages to Yedo but they went in the humiliating character of bearers of tribute and were treated as prisoners. This would be the first time a foreigner had visited Yedo in any other character. His journey would form a precedent which would be followed when other diplomats come to the Shogun's capital. It was important as well as difficult to settle all of the details correctly. Two officers would leave in a few days for Yedo to assist in making the arrangements there while those who remained in Shimoda would consult with Harris and assist in his preparations. With the Japanese genius for elaborate stage-settings and their passion for precedent, the details of what was to be a triumphal journey for Harris caused many days of anxious study on the part of the Yedo officials.

As the plans developed, it became more and more apparent that this brief journey was to be made with the traditional Oriental pomp and splendor, the like of which no American had ever dreamed of. In addition to the forty-odd porters who would carry the luggage, bedding and cooking utensils, there were to be the following uniformed attendants attached to Harris' retinue:

- 20 palanquin-bearers
- 12 guardsmen
- 2 standard-bearers
- 2 shoe- and fan-bearers
- 2 grooms
- 2 commanders who would have charge of the others

The palanquin-bearers and grooms were to wear a single sword but the others were to wear the two swords of the *samurai.* All were to wear silk robes of special design on which would appear, at the suggestion of Harris, the embroidered coat-of-arms of the United States. With Mr. Heusken and the Japanese cook and butler this made a company of more than eighty people. The American entourage was to be escorted to the capital by the Vice-Governor and other officials with their attendants, so that altogether the parade which would comprise about 250 people would be as pretentious as that which accompanied the most important of feudal princes on their official journeys to Yedo.

As the preparations for the great journey continued Harris found his health greatly improved. He attributed this partly to the fact that he now had a good supply of "delicate China pork." His sow had farrowed thirteen pigs on August 5; he had given two of these pigs to the officers of the *Portsmouth*. While the fresh pork helped to bring back his health he

had no doubt that the agreeable termination of the vexed question of the reception of the President's letter has also been of great service to me as it has removed an immense pressure from my mind. I cannot help hoping that I shall be able to do something satisfactory in the way of a commercial treaty before I leave Yedo.

But his birthday which came while these preparations were in progress brought grim forebodings to his mind.

I am fifty-three years old. My lease is rapidly running to its close. God grant that the short remainder of it may be usefully and honorably employed. My health is better than it was a month ago but far, very far, from being good as it was this time last year. Shall I ever see New York and my dear American friends again? *Doubtful,* but God's will be done, I can say truly and heartily.

186

How foolish these dire forebodings were may be seen by the fact that he lived for another twenty years.

The weeks of preparation for the trip were busily and pleasantly occupied. The Yedo officials had evidently given very strict orders that the arrangements must be to his satisfaction, for almost every day he was called on to confirm some detail or settle some disputed point. There was no doubt but that it was to be his party. For the first time his relations with the governors were completely friendly. They played the part of generous and considerate hosts, while he was the appreciative guest.

Always very particular about his own clothing, he personally supervised the making of the many ceremonial silk garments which his attendants were to wear to Yedo. He had several complete outfits made so that when they reached the capital the travel-stained garments could be replaced by fresh ones. He also had a new American flag made of Japanese silk. When the job of making the clothing was completed he was able to record the fact that the work was satisfactory. The coat-of-arms with which every suit was embellished was very neatly done and the motto *E pluribus unum*, the eagle, arrows and olive branch were embroidered perfectly. It was the first time he had expressed unqualified approval of any product of Japanese workmanship. It was also the first time the coat-of-arms of the United States had appeared on a Japanese ceremonial gown.

The question of presents for the Shogun and Ministers of Yedo afforded some difficulties. The Department of State had loaded the *San Jacinto* with a pretentious and varied assortment of presents for the two Kings of Siam, but apparently they had not thought it necessary to provide anything for Japan after the very lavish gifts which Commo-

dore Perry had taken with him. The department officials
did not know that Oriental etiquette demanded another lot
of gifts for Harris to present.

Harris searched through his belongings and packed up
what he could find. Having noted the gusto with which the
local Japanese officials consumed his drinks he assumed that
liquor would be acceptable and his wine cellar was well
stocked. He had not had a drink since leaving Marseilles
and in the absence of ships, there had been few calls on
his hospitality. He made up a good assortment of champagne, sherry, cordials, cherry brandy and table wines.
There was an established precedent for alcoholic gifts.
Perry had brought with him a whole barrel of rye whisky
for the Emperor. More substantial presents Harris was able
to find in his store included a telescope, a barometer, astral
lamp, cut-glass decanters and books. One might be justified
in assuming that some of these things had been intended
for the Kings of Siam and that Harris had held out on
them in order to meet the obligations which he knew would
face him in Japan.

In the midst of these preparations a Japanese junk which
had sailed from Hakodate brought him a parcel of mail
from America. There were a few circulars from the Department of State but no letters. There was not one word from
the department about the treaty which he had negotiated
with Siam, but from personal letters he learned that only
a few days after his arrival in Japan he had narrowly escaped
a somewhat humiliating dismissal from office.

It appears that the treaty reached Washington on the 17th
of September, 1856, and on the same day the New York *Times*
published what it said was the actual treaty. The President
held that it was I and I alone that communicated it to the

*Times*, and was for my instant removal. This was prevented only by the friendship of Secretary Marcy and the untiring labours of my kind friend, General Wetmore.

This news, coming after the long neglect by the officials at Washington, upset him so completely that he filled several pages of his journal with comments about it. By comparing the text of the treaty with the text as published he showed that the correspondent of the New York *Times* could not even have seen the correct text.

The President appeared to think the best mode of proceeding would be to punish me first, and *then* ask me for my defence. This mode of procedure is quite common among Oriental despots, but I am inclined to think that the Western rule is to hold every man innocent until he is proved to be guilty. Had the President, in his ardent desire to punish the guilty, given orders to compare the publication in the *Times* with the official copy in the State Department, he would at once have seen that the *Times* version could not have emanated from me, nor from anyone who had an opportunity of copying the Treaty!!!

On October 28 Moriyama returned from Yedo with further information about official plans for the visit to Yedo. With their usual punctilious regard for everything connected with a ceremonial observance, the Japanese had prepared a ground plan of the buildings in which the audience was to take place. The whole program was explained in detail to Harris and was approved by him with one exception.

They proposed that, after my audience was over and I had retired, I should return to the Audience Chamber, not as the representative of the President, but in my private capacity; that instead of proceeding to the place I formerly occupied, I should stop at the place where I made my first bow; that the Ziogoon would address me, to which I was not to reply, but simply bow and retire.

It struck me that there was some petty scheme of glorifying themselves at my expense in this proposition, and I avoided it by saying that I could not divest myself of my character of plenipotentiary which had been conferred on me by the President, and that, so long as the President pleased, I must maintain that character. They were evidently chagrined at this and tried to persuade me to alter my decision, assuring me that it was meant as a personal favor to me, etc. I replied that I was gratified for the intention; and that if the Ziogoon wished to see me at a private audience, I would cheerfully attend him, but that it must always be in my official character.

As the time for departure for Yedo was approaching, the Shimoda officials found it necessary to prepare him for the monumental deception for which the visit to Yedo was to provide the stage-setting. They told him that the proper title of their ruler was not Ziogoon, which meant literally "generalissimo," but Tycoon, or "great ruler." The title of Tycoon had in fact been invented for the occasion solely for the purpose of further obscuring the fact that the Shogun was not the Emperor of the country.

The genius of the people shines out in this. For more than a year I have spoken and written Ziogoon when referring to their ruler, and they never gave me any explanation; but now, when I am on the eve of starting for Yedo, they give the real word.

Leaving for Yedo involved the actual closing of the consulate as of course Heusken would have to go with Harris to serve as interpreter. He had no idea how long he would be gone nor what ships might call during his absence, so he prepared and left with the Shimoda officials two letters, one to be delivered to any United States naval commander and the other to the captain of any merchant vessel who might call at Shimoda. A third document left with the officials was a warrant empowering them to arrest and hold his Chinese servants if they should attempt to leave Shimoda during his absence. None of the three letters was ever used as no ships called and the Chinese servants had no opportunity to escape.

At the last moment the Japanese added an enormous umbrella to the procession. This was a significant addition, for those huge umbrellas were carried only in the entourage of princes of the highest rank.

## CHAPTER XVIII

## THE GREAT JOURNEY TO YEDO

O N MONDAY, November 23, 1857, Townsend Harris felt
in much better health than he had for a long time. All
his past ills were forgotten in an exultation of spirit which
made them appear small and unimportant. He was on the
eve of the greatest adventure of his life—was setting out for
Yedo. The day dawned bright and clear, just the sort of
day anyone would wish for when about to undertake a
journey. The wooded hills were sharply cut against a cloud-
less sky and the sea below was a brightly shining azure mir-
ror. He was up at sunrise to see that everything was in order,
and at 8 o'clock he was on his way to the mysterious Yedo,
traveling as no foreigner had ever before traveled in Japan,
for he was the center of a colorful ceremony reserved for
princes of the blood.

A mile from the temple his procession joined the main
cavalcade and he was able to see for the first time the pageant
which had been in preparation for more than two months.
In his many weary and lonely walks he had been over this
route before but now it had quite a different aspect. The
wide pathway had been repaired and swept clean and all
the underbrush cut away from the sides and bridges built
over the tiny streams. It was as tidy as a pathway in a park.
The country people who were out to see the pageant had
washed their faces and put on their ceremonial clothing.
At the head of the procession went three lads carrying

decorated wands of bamboo, who alternately cried out the spectators along the route: *"staneo-hiro"* (please down), the different tones of the three voices forming a strange but pleasant musical chorus. The chant was never broken, even when they passed along deserted stretches of the road. This was the only human sound to be heard. Following the boys came the new American flag, escorted by a military officer and flanked by two strapping guards on whose silk coats were embroidered the coat-of-arms of the United States.

This was the preliminary setting for the appearance of Harris himself, with his six uniformed guards, his horse and grooms, his palanquin with its twelve bearers and the bearers of his shoes and fan, each dressed in distinctive costume. Mr. Heusken followed with his own guards and palanquin. There were dozens of porters carrying bedding, trunks and kitchen utensils. Each package was carefully wrapped and decorated with the coat-of-arms of the United States or had a small American flag flying from a bamboo standard. The tall palanquin-bearers wore a costume and insignia allowed only to those who were privileged to carry princes. The rear of the procession was composed of the Shimoda officials with their guards and attendants, fewer in number and lower in rank than those who attended Harris. The whole train consisted of no less than 350 people.

The cavalcade traveled with leisurely dignity. There were frequent halts to change the porters and palanquin-bearers and a long stop for the midday meal. The palanquin-bearers had an easy time of it so far as the two Americans were concerned, for during the first part of the journey both Harris and Heusken rode their horses. At the end of the first day, having covered fifteen miles, they stopped at a small village where a temple had been prepared as quarters for Harris by the installation of a private bathroom and toilet.

The news that the great American "Ambassador" was going to make a ceremonial journey to the capital had spread throughout Japan very soon after the Yedo officials came to their decision to invite him. As a news-event it aroused as much interest as the appearance of Perry's "black ship" in the Bay of Yedo, and was subject to as much exaggerated speculation. Thousands of crudely printed leaflets giving fanciful pictures of the journey had been sold throughout the country and the subject was discussed in every village. For centuries the Japanese had watched the ceremonial processions of princes on the way to or from the capital, but the visit of one of those strange and mysterious Americans promised a new and even more thrilling sensation. The fact that this great man was a countryman of the sea-captain whose black ships had thrown terror into all Japan added a sinister fascination in the minds of the superstitious country people. Perry's visit had been followed by the death of the Shogun and earthquakes and tidal waves of unusual violence, indicating to many that the gods were wrathful. Would this visit of the American Consul-General to the capital itself be followed by similar disturbances?

The first part of the route was through the countryside with its small isolated villages and it was not until the third day of the journey that the crowds began to appear. The procession now was traveling over the great imperial road between Kyoto and Yedo and at all the stopping places the shops, except those selling food, were closed. The streets were crowded with visitors, some of whom had left their homes a week before and had traveled a hundred miles. There were stupid country people and a goodly sprinkling of the proud sword-bearing *samurai* who gave no hint of their hatred for this barbarian intruder. All were orderly and well behaved and showed the same respectful deference they had been accustomed to show in the presence of princes of the most powerful families. There was no jostling or shouting or noise of any kind, not even the subdued monotone of a crowd as heard from a distance. The only distinguishable sound was that of the three heralds with their musical chant, "Sit down, please! Sit down, please! Sit down, please!"

As Harris passed all knelt down with averted eyes "as though they were not worthy even to look at me. Only those of a certain rank were allowed to salute me, which was done by *knocking head* or bringing the forehead actually to the ground." Only the girls took sly looks at him. At the border of each village he was met by the local authorities who were waiting to escort him through their territory. Each change of escort was made the occasion of a colorful little ceremony, old and new escorts prostrating themselves before the American. He had traveled a long way from the chinaware shop in Pearl Street!

Along the imperial highway there were even more comfortable lodging places and rest houses, and Harris was given the use of those reserved for princes of the highest rank— places surrounded with such dignity that even the Vice-Governor of Shimoda could not stop in them. Harris was very comfortable in these places, but there were many points on the journey where he would have been glad to dispense with some of the dignity. The palanquin represented the height of distinction—and also the depth of discomfort to an American who was unaccustomed to sitting in Japanese style with his legs folded up like the blades of a jack-knife. He had had a palanquin specially built with plenty of leg room so that he could ride in it lying down in tolerable comfort instead of squatting on his heels. He rode his horse wherever possible but on the mountain roads he had to lie down on the hard floor of the palanquin and be carried over the edge of precipices. He would have much preferred to walk but his exalted position did not allow it.

The great road was thirty to forty feet wide and bordered by huge pines, camphor and cryptomeria trees, some of which had been broken by the typhoon which followed the visit of Perry. At times the road climbed high in the hills and at others skirted the seashore. Each turn brought new views of the always-enchanting Japanese landscape—groves of pine and bamboo, cascading waterfalls or little streams which raced by under beautiful old stone bridges. Ordinarily this highway was crowded with porters carrying cargo— for it was the only great highway in the country—but the cavalcade passed no traffic as the road had been reserved for its use. Only thousands of people dressed in their best ceremonial costumes knelt by the roadside and either humbly looked downward or pressed their foreheads to the ground.

The places where the procession made brief halts to change the palanquin-bearers had been carefully selected and marked by long streamers of bunting of black and white—the imperial colors. The cross-roads and paths leading to the imperial highway were all closed off by ropes. The entrance to each village was marked by small cones of earth surmounted by a sprig of green. At each stopping-place a stake was provided to which the flagstaff bearing the American flag could be attached.

In spite of all that had been done to make the journey

to Yedo a pleasant one, the tangled mass of red tape with which official Japan was encumbered had not been cleared away. When the journey was more than half completed Harris ran into one of the many troublesome police regulations, entailing a conflict of authority, which have harassed foreign visitors from his day to this. As they approached the pass leading to the Yedo district

the Vice-Governor of Shimoda, after a vast deal of circumlocution, informed me that, when the great princes of the Empire passed here, the door of the *norimon* (palanquin) was opened and an officer looked into it, without stopping the bearers; that it was a mere ceremony, but the ancient laws required it, etc., etc.

I replied that, as I was not a Japanese subject, and being as I was the diplomatic representative of the United States, I was free from any such search; that they knew what was in my *norimon*, and could inform the officers at the pass that there was nothing forbidden in it. The Vice-Governor tried for some time to change my determination, and at last proposed that I should ride through on horseback, and then permit the search of the empty *norimon*. I decidedly declined this, telling him that it was the search under *any form* that I objected to. He then said we must stop until he could send to Yedo for instructions which would only take five days. I told him I should not wait five days nor five hours; that if the search was insisted on I should at once return to Shimoda. The poor Vice-Governor was in great tribulation and finally went to the guard-house and after a delay of two hours returned with word that it was all settled and that I should pass unmolested.

The vicious horse Harris rode provided another upset for the carefully prepared plans.

As I mounted my horse after being ferried over the Banu-gawa, my vicious brute of a horse both bit and kicked me. The little finger of my left hand was very painful and I ordered some leeches to be applied. The doctor approached with great trepidation, while large drops of perspiration stood on his forehead. I asked what ailed him; he said he had never approached any person of such exalted rank before, and he was terrified at the idea of drawing blood from me. He was told to forget all about rank, and to apply his remedy as quickly as possible. . . . My surgeon having finished his labor, retired a proud and happy man; happy that he had pleased me, and proud that he had been called on to attend a person occupying my position.

As they approached nearer to Yedo the villages became larger and more frequent, and the increasing number of people who crowded the roadway on either side lent a metropolitan air to the proceedings. The village authorities here were supported by a body of local policemen each of whom carried a heavy iron staff to which four or five rings were attached. With each alternate step the rod was struck on the ground and the musical jingle of the iron rings gave notice to the populace to kneel.

On Saturday afternoon the procession arrived at Kawasaki where it was to halt until Monday, as Harris had made it clear that he refused to travel on Sunday or to transact any business on that day. Here he found the first apparent carelessness in carrying out the arrangements for his journey for the *honjin* or rest house where he was to spend the week-end was in a dilapidated condition. Doors and windows would not close, the paper window-panes in many places were broken, so that the wind played freely through the rooms, while an air of dirty slovenliness reigned over the whole. He was particularly surprised and annoyed because this was the first instance of a dirty house he had seen in Japan.

This inhospitable reception may have been caused by carelessness on the part of the local authorities, but it is much more probable that it was part of a carefully prepared plan to provide quarters so uncomfortable that Harris would break his resolution about the observance of Sunday and push on to Yedo. This would have brought him to the capital on Sunday and would have been, in the Japanese eyes, a very clever maneuver: it would have proven that the resolution Harris had shown in all of his dealings with them could be broken. If they could succeed in this then they would feel free to adopt a bolder course in the negotiations at Yedo. However, if such was their plan, it failed completely, for Heusken was sent at once to look for other lodgings and soon returned with word that he had found a hotel that was neat, clean, comfortable and pleasantly located. The Japanese officials were horrified. The fact that the quarters they had provided for their distinguished guest were so filthy that he was compelled to move into an inn involved a disgraceful loss of prestige which was sure to be followed by dangerous repercussions from the officials at Yedo.

The Vice-Governor implored me not to think of going to a tavern, but, rather than I should do so, he would give up his quarters and go to the tavern himself. I told him I could not think of disturbing him; and, as to my dignity, *that* was my affair, and I would take good care of it. . . . Among other reasons advanced by the Governor was the very grave fact that at all the *honjins* the floor of the room occupied by me was raised some three inches higher than the other rooms; that to place me on a floor of the same level as the others was to derogate from the respect due to me; that the most positive orders had been issued by the Tycoon that I should receive all the marks of honor on my journey that were bestowed on persons of the most exalted rank in Japan, and for that reason I had always been lodged in *honjins* on a raised floor which was covered with mats of the finest quality and bordered with a binding of a particular pattern, etc., etc. I answered him that what he said was no doubt very true and very proper, but he had forgotten that I sat on chairs that raised me much higher than even the favored floor of the *honjin*, and that as to the mats and binding my being a foreigner would allow me to dispense with those considerations while I was in Kawasaki, and so *that* matter ended after consuming nearly three hours.

The day following his arrival in Kawasaki was the first Sunday in Advent and he held extempory church services in his room in the tavern, reading the whole Protestant Episcopal service from his prayer book with Heusken as the clerk and congregation.

I experienced some peculiar feelings on this occasion. It was beyond doubt the first time that ever a Christian service on the Sabbath was read audibly in this place, which is only thirteen miles from Yedo, and this, too, while the law punishing such an act with death is still in force.*

On leaving Kawasaki, Harris turned his horse over to a groom and proceeded all the way in his uncomfortable palanquin. He had suggested riding the horse the remainder of the route to Yedo, but the eagerness with which the Vice-Governor had encouraged this idea aroused his suspicions. After considerable difficulty he learned that only princes of the highest rank could enter Yedo in their palanquins, those of secondary rank being allowed to ride on horseback while

* While the strict laws against the Christian religion had not been repealed it was not exactly correct to say that they were in force. After the visit of Perry they were conveniently forgotten and the Dutch convention signed at Nagasaki on January 30, 1856, provided that the Dutch could practice the Christian religion.

200

all others walked. Again he had to choose between dignity and comfort and he rode in the palanquin.

The glorious weather under which the journey had started continued all the way from Shimoda to Yedo. Instead of the gods manifesting their disapproval, the journey was made under the most convincing manifestations of beneficence. Not a drop of rain fell and not a single cloud obscured the sun. The new silk flag was as fresh as it had been the day they started. It was delightfully cool. Harris was so entranced by his strange surroundings and new experiences that he forgot to note that he spent Thanksgiving Day en route.

On Monday, the last day of the journey, the villages forming the suburbs of Yedo were so close together as to make an almost continuous street. As the procession approached the imperial city it was reformed. The Vice-Governor now led the way, the coolies and porters keeping to a kind of military formation; the cavalcade of nearly half a mile proceeded at the slow and stately step required of those nearing the precincts of the ruler of Japan. Here the retainers of the *daimyos* who lined the street remained standing but with eyes cast to the ground. At every intersection of a main street—distances of about 120 yards—the guard of honor was changed, new local officials took up the responsibility of escorting the travelers to the next intersection where Harris was received with prostrations and knocking of heads.

Every cross street had its stockade closed to prevent too great a crowd; and, as I looked up and down those streets, they seemed a solid mass of men and women. The most perfect order was maintained from Sinigawa to my lodgings—a distance of over seven miles. Not a shout or cry was heard. The silence of such a vast multitude had something appalling in it.

Harris estimated the number of people at each intersection and from that made a rough calculation that the number of persons who lined the streets was no less than 184,000. This did not include the thousands who were jammed into the side streets or had clambered to the tops of houses.

At length the procession passed the Nihonbashi, the great Bridge of Japan, the point from which all distances in the Empire were measured, then traveled along a moat and came to the walls of the great Castle of Yedo. As they approached the gate the palanquin-bearers broke into a run, rushed through the gateway, across a courtyard and into the house itself before the palanquin was lowered to the ground.

The highest prince in the Empire could not have entered Yedo in a more honorable manner.

## CHAPTER XIX

## HONORED GUEST OF THE SHOGUN

WHEN the "American Ambassador" entered the house which had been provided for him inside the great castle at Yedo he found it much more carefully and comfortably equipped than the quarters given him in Bangkok. In his bedroom and sitting-room were exact duplicates of the furniture from his house in Shimoda. In an adjoining room was a water-closet which was also a duplicate. Special artisans had been sent from Yedo to Shimoda to make copies of these articles. It was the first time any such unusual pieces of furniture had been seen in the capital city. According to a story which was current in Tokyo many years later the Japanese artisans did their work so faithfully that they reproduced a broken table leg and all the other defects they had found in the Shimoda temple.

The rather spacious building which was turned over to Harris had been used as the "Office for the Examination of Barbarian Books." It was here that books published in foreign countries were read by a board of censors; only those which received official approval were allowed to be translated and published. The feverish search for Western learning had just begun but had been placed under the strict official surveillance which has never been lifted. Most of the books examined were in the Dutch language and the only ones which were treated liberally by the censors were works on medicine. Even the study of foreign languages was prohibited. In consequence thousands of young Japanese secured permission to study Dutch on the pretext that they wished to become physicians. The "barbarian" classification did not apply to Chinese books and they were freely circulated. Japan still looked on China as the fountainhead of all knowledge and culture and the classical Japanese education was confined to a study of Chinese history and the Confucian philosophy. Japan's first knowledge of American history had come through Chinese books.

In these strange surroundings Harris was greeted as an old friend by the Prince of Shinano who made anxious inquiries about the journey and told him about the further plans for his entertainment. Eight persons of distinguished rank had been appointed as "Commissioners of the Voyage of the American Ambassador to Yedo." The Prince explained that their principal duties were to make his visit as pleasant and comfortable as possible. But Harris had reason to believe that they had been appointed because of their diplomatic experience rather than because of their hospitable talents. Included in the list of eight were the two commissioners who had negotiated the treaty with Perry. A third had assisted in the negotiation of the treaty with Russia. And the slippery Moriyama was to be in attendance to take care of the translations and assume the blame for anything that went wrong.

Although there were only eight commissioners, they were accompanied by a retinue of several hundred when they called on Harris the next day for a formal presentation.

Each one had his pikes, or ensigns of his dignity, borne before him, and led horses followed his *norimon*. The caparisons of the horses bore the coat of arms of the noble owner. Among others each "following" had fan bearers, slipper bearers, cane bearers, etc. Each had his *camissimo* or dress of ceremony brought with him in neat lacquered boxes, and his portfolio was neatly wrapped in silk and slung over the back of a particular bearer. After they arrived they went at once to rooms where they put on their *camissimos,* and then they proceeded to the Audience Chamber.

In private letters Harris refers to all their ostentation as being repugnant to his republican tastes but in his journal he set down every detail with evident relish.

At every turn he was introduced to some new phase of the complicated etiquette of the country, beside which that of Siam appeared simplicity itself. Each ruling, seemingly, was designed to explain some delay. The Prince of Tamba, the ambassador who acted as the personal representative of the Shogun, did not call on Harris at once and it was explained that he

was delayed by the wish of His Majesty to examine personally the present, which, by the laws of etiquette of Japan, was to be presented to me by the Tycoon; and he then added that, after it had been examined in the Palace, it had to be taken to the Great Council for their examination. In answer to my inquiries, I was told that the Tycoon cannot make or receive the smallest presents until they have been examined and approved by the Council of State!!! That single statement convinced me that the Tycoon was a mere "lay figure" of government, and that he did not possess a single particle of political power.

On the later visit of the Prince of Tamba the American learned still more about the complexities of the Japanese etiquette. When the official spoke about or for the Shogun he stood on a slightly raised platform of the audience chamber, but when he answered a personal inquiry which concerned himself alone he stepped down to a lower level.

When the present was mentioned he turned toward it and bowed. The requirements of etiquette kept him hopping from one level to the other throughout the conversation, while Harris remained at one level—just like the barbarian that he was in the Japanese eyes. When the present which had been so carefully examined was brought in it was found to consist of about seventy pounds of Japanese bon-bons which Harris was afraid to eat.

The Prince of Shinano took to himself most of the credit for having made the arrangements for Harris' visit to the capital.

He enlarged on the difficulties he had overcome and the great labor he had performed to enable me to come to Yedo. He spoke of his anxious days and sleepless nights; that care and anxiety had taken away his appetite, so that he had become lean in his person; and that the blood frequently gushed from his nose from his great agitation; that he had done all this from his friendship for me, etc.

Harris was quite reasonably suspicious of this attempt to place him under personal obligations and set the matter right at once.

I replied that I was duly grateful to him for his friendship for me; but, as he appeared to be under a great error as far as it regarded my visit to Yedo, I must now fully explain myself on that point. I told him that I came to Yedo as the representative of the United States, and not in my private capacity; that the United States did not ask anything from the Government of Japan *as a favor*; that it only demanded its rights, and that nothing would be accepted on the ground of favor; that my mission had for its object the good of the Japanese Empire; and that it was no favor to me or my country that they should listen to my advice, but that it was the Japanese who should feel grateful to the President for the friendship he had shown to Japan by the messages with which I was entrusted.

That for myself, individually, I had no wish to come to Yedo, and that I only came here because my official duty required it; that I hoped he now fully understood not only my object in visiting Yedo, but that he would clearly see that it was not any favor to me either in my private or in my official capacity to receive me at Yedo.

The Prince was quite chopfallen at this, as it was the evident wish of the Japanese that I should look on my reception as an unprecedented favor to me, both personally and officially, and thus they would establish a claim on my gratitude, which might be of great use to them in the negotiations that might be commenced here.

In passing it may be remarked that Harris' attitude—his consistent refusal to allow his relations with the Japanese officials to be placed on a personal basis—was quite different from that of Commodore Perry who on a good many occasions had listened complacently to Japanese assurances that the greatly exaggerated concessions they made to the American government were because of personal regard for him.

Now that Harris was in Yedo the officials had to redouble their efforts to continue the pretense that the Shogun and the Emperor were one and the same person. Everyone in Japan knew exactly what the situation was, but the deception of foreigners appears to have been complete. In his journal Harris refers to the Shogun as the Tycoon, the new title invented by the Japanese officials. But in personal letters he referred to him as the Emperor. In order to make sure that this deception was carried out it was necessary that every precaution be taken to prevent either Heusken or Harris from making informal visits to the city of Yedo.

They were warned that there were many bad people about who might insult them and thus cause serious difficulties. Harris' insistence that he must be permitted some physical exercise threw his official hosts into a ferment of anxiety.

The first few days were filled with receiving visits and paying calls on the Yedo officials, and although these did not involve anything more than a journey from one part of the castle to another Harris was attended by the retinue which had accompanied him from Shimoda. Only the cook, butler and the porters remained behind. On reaching the gateway to the residence of the official on whom he was calling, the palanquin-bearers always dashed through at full speed. There were the invariable punctilious inquiries about the health of Harris and the President of the United States. Harris had to draw on his imagination to answer any question about the health of President Harrison for he had heard nothing from Washington for more than a year. Inquiries about the health of the Shogun might have been equally embarrassing to the Japanese officials had a frank answer been expected for he was wasting away from an hereditary disease and was to die within a year.

It is perhaps fortunate that the Japanese did not prosecute their inquiries very thoroughly. If they had known that President Pierce who signed the letter to the Emperor had been repudiated by his own party and was now out of power it might have provided them with new pretexts. But nothing interfered with the movement of events according to the schedule which had been arranged. At his call on the Prime Minister Harris was told that he would be received by the Shogun on Monday, December 7. Events were moving with satisfactory speed for he had arrived in Yedo on the last day of November.

On the occasion of the audience which he thought was with the Emperor of Japan Harris put on the gold laced uniform which he had packed away on leaving Siam. Mr. Heusken wore an undress navy uniform with a sword and cocked hat. They were brought to the audience chamber a full hour early so as to have time for a rehearsal which the Yedo officials insisted was necessary. But Harris firmly declined, saying that he was quite familiar with court ceremonies of Europe and required no coaching.

In the hall leading to the audience chamber there were 300 to 400 Japanese nobles kneeling as motionless as statues. The spectacle was less gaudy and more impressive than the one he had seen in Siam. The Japanese officials were all in court dress, the most striking garment being the trousers of yellow silk with legs six or seven feet long. When the wearer walked the ends of the legs streamed out behind him, so giving him the appearance of walking humbly on his knees. In the audience chamber itself this pretense of humbleness was not enough and all the *daimyos*, including the highest and most powerful princes, prostrated themselves, just as the princes of Siam had done. The Prince of Shinano, who acted as Harris' escort, crawled along on his hands and knees while Harris walked beside him. The American undoubtedly would have found some humor in the situation had he known that the person to whom the princes of Japan were showing such deference had been selected as Shogun because he was so weak-minded that he was the easily controlled tool of the very men who were now prostrating themselves before him.

As Harris entered the audience chamber and paused, a chamberlain called out in a loud voice:

"Embassador Merican!"

Harris bowed, proceeded nearly to the middle of the room where he halted in front of the raised platform on which the Shogun was seated, and bowed again. On both sides of him were prostrate princes, their foreheads pressed to the floor. These same princes, only a short time before this, had given the Shogun explicit directions as to what he was to do and had written the speech he was to make. After a third and final bow Harris addressed the Shogun as follows:

"May it please Your Majesty:

"In presenting my letters of credence from the President of the United States, I am directed to express to Your Majesty the sincere wishes of the President for your health and happiness and for the prosperity of your dominions. I consider it a great honor that I have been selected to fill the high and important place of Plenipotentiary of the United States at the Court of Your Majesty; and, as my earnest wishes are to unite the two countries more closely in the ties of enduring friendship, my constant exertions shall be directed to the attainment of that happy end."

The speech was brief enough but was positively verbose as compared with the reply of the Shogun. He jerked his head back over his left shoulder, stamped his foot several times in an imperious gesture and then uttered a few words which were translated as follows:

"Pleased with the letter sent with the Ambassador from a far distant country, and likewise pleased with his discourse. Intercourse shall be continued forever."

The speech in translation was even longer than in the original for it consisted of less than twenty Japanese words. As Harris' address and the Shogun's curt reply had been translated and exchanged a few days before the audience, neither was interpreted.

Mr. Heusken, who had been standing at the door of the audience chamber, then advanced and with three bows to the Shogun gave the letter of President Pierce to Harris who presented it to the Shogun through the Minister of Foreign Affairs. The letter read as follows:

To His Majesty the Emperor of Japan.
Great and Good Friend:
It has occurred to me that the existing treaty between the United States and Japan might be amended so as to secure greater facilities for the exchange of the rich and varied productions of Your Majesty's vast empire for those of the United States. I have accordingly made choice of the bearer of this letter, Townsend Harris, Esquire, a citizen of this country, who has already been accredited to Your Majesty's Minister for Foreign Affairs as the Consul-General of the United States, to confer upon the subject with such ministers or other officers as Your Majesty may designate. I trust that they may agree upon the terms of a treaty which will strengthen and perpetuate the bonds of amity between the United States and Japan as well as increase the commercial intercourse between them to their mutual advantage.

I trust that Your Majesty will receive Mr. Harris with kindness and will place entire confidence in all the representations which he may make to Your Majesty in my behalf.

I pray God to have Your Majesty in His safe and holy keeping.

To these presents I have caused the seal of the United States to be affixed and have subscribed the same with my hand, at the city of Washington, on the twelfth day of September, in the year of the Christian Era, one thousand, eight hundred and fifty-five.

FRANKLIN PIERCE

By the President:
W. L. Marcy, Secretary of State.

After this brief formal audience was over there was more petty diplomatic maneuvering designed to impress on Harris the great honor that had been shown him by the Shogun and also to warn him against any further attempts at intimacy with so great a personage. The Japanese officials congratulated him on the marvelous self-possession he had shown, saying he had given evidence of a true "greatness of soul," for he had not "trembled and quaked" in the presence of the mighty ruler of Japan.

A good deal of negotiation had been used by the Japanese to get me to eat a dinner at the Palace alone or with Mr. Heusken only. This I declined doing. I offered to partake of it provided one of the Royal Family or the Prime Minister would eat with me. I was told that their customs forbade either from doing so. I replied that the customs of my country forbade anyone to eat in a house where the host or his representative did not sit down to table with him. At last the matter was arranged by ordering the dinner to be sent to my lodgings.

It was a marvelous dinner, beautifully decorated with miniature fir trees and many longevity emblems of storks and tortoises. But Harris could not eat a morsel of it. He had caught a violent cold in the audience chamber and was shaking with a chill. A Japanese doctor gave him hot drinks and put him to bed.

## CHAPTER XX

## SOME ADVICE TO THE JAPANESE

THE day following the audience with the Shogun Harris was still sick but was well enough to write a letter to Lord Hotta, the Minister of Foreign Affairs, stating that he had some important communications to make which were of deep concern to Japan; which he would transmit either to him or to the whole Council of State. Prior to Harris' arrival in Yedo this body had been increased in number from five to six so that Lord Hotta could devote his entire attention to the duties of Minister of Foreign Affairs. This was in fact the beginning of the formation of the modern cabinet of Japan which has played such an important part in the government of the country.

Harris also sent to the Shogun the rather pitiful presents he had been able to bring from Shimoda. They consisted of sixty bottles of liquors of various sorts, an "astral" lamp, two decanters, telescope, barometer, a book on natural history and five padlocks. The whole lot did not make a load heavy enough to burden one porter. The gifts Perry had brought had been so numerous and pretentious that a special pavilion had been built to house them. After Harris had unpacked the gifts and checked them over he was told that it would be impolite to send them except on ceremonial trays so these were made at considerable expense, adding to his steadily mounting indebtedness to the Japanese officials.

He was not given an opportunity to deliver his message to the Council of State but Lord Hotta was commissioned to receive it, assisted by the "commissioners of the voyage." The meeting with Lord Hotta which was arranged for Saturday, December 12, provided the opportunity which Harris had been seeking since his arrival in Japan to lay before the responsible Japanese authorities the ideas he had regarding the foreign problems of the country and the policy they should follow. It was a subject on which he could speak with more sincerity than a diplomat usually employs, for he believed that in proposing his program to the Japanese he was not only performing his duty to his own country but also serving the best interests of the country to which he was accredited. During his long isolation at Shimoda he had had plenty of time to go over the matter in his own mind and he had in fact written a detailed memorandum of all he proposed to say.

His statement to the council, with the necessary translation into Dutch and then into Japanese, consumed about two hours.

I commenced [he says*] by assuring the Minister of the friendly feelings of the President towards Japan and that my government had no wish to acquire any territory in the East. . . . I stated that the introduction of steam navigation had produced great changes during the last fifty years; that nations which before that time were separated by wide oceans were now brought within a few days of each other; that commercial intercourse had thereby greatly increased adding to the national wealth of each country and to the happiness of the people; that the chief Western powers fostered commerce as one of the great sources of national prosperity.

* From Harris' record of his conversation in the archives of the American Embassy at Tokyo.

I stated that the discovery of rich gold mines in California had led to the rapid population of the West Coast of the United States. . . . That the completion of a railway that would unite the East and West Coast was only a matter of time. . . . I said the Islands of Japan are in the direct line between the West Coast of the United States and the East Coast of Asia and that a great and constantly increasing intercourse with Japan would arise thereby. I said that Japan would by the operation of these things be compelled to abandon her exclusive policy and that she might soon become a great and powerful nation by simply permitting her people to exercise their ingenuity and industry; that the resources of Japan when developed by the action of trade would show a vast amount of exchangeable values; that this production would not interfere with the production of the necessary food for the people but would arise from the employment given to the actual surplus labor of the country. . . .

I added that by negotiating with me, unsupported as I was by any force whatever, the honor of Japan would not be injured; that each point could be deliberately discussed and considered and preparations made for opening the country gradually. On the subject of religion I stated that the principle of leaving men free to follow the dictates of their own consciences was adopted in most of the countries of the West and that in all cases it ensured the peace and happiness of the country. . . . I said that a satisfactory commercial treaty could be based on three points: 1) The residence of a diplomatic representative at Yedo. 2) Freedom of trade with the Japanese without the interference of government officials. 3) The opening of additional harbors.

Having pointed out with what can now be described as prophetic vision the advantages which would accrue to Japan from the opening up of the country, he next turned to a logical statement of the consequences she might expect if she persisted in her policy of exclusion. He said that foreign nations would, one after another, send powerful fleets to Japan to demand the opening of the country; that Japan must either yield or suffer the miseries of war; that, even if war did not ensue, the country would be kept in a constant state of excitement by the presence of these large foreign armaments; that to make a concession of any value it must be in due season. He specifically mentioned Great Britain and told of that country's plans to send a powerful fleet to Japan to enforce the signing of a treaty as soon as the pressing problems in China had been liquidated. This information about the plans of Great Britain was all the more convincing because it was not new to the Japanese but served to confirm information they had received from the Dutch.

Harris' presentation of the case led to the point he hoped to make, which was that "the terms demanded by a fleet would never be as moderate as those asked by a person placed as I was; and that to yield to a fleet what was refused to an ambassador would humiliate the government in the eyes of all the Japanese people, and thus actually weaken its power."

Then he recalled the humiliating story of China whose Manchu rulers had insultingly rejected the overtures of foreign powers and later had been compelled to sign a treaty under the guns of a victorious fleet. They had failed to respect that treaty, and now at the moment he was speaking, a still more powerful fleet had sailed north to the Gulf of Pechili and was prepared to send armed forces to Peking itself. Whether or not the logical arguments he presented were convincing to the Japanese, there can be no doubt but that they were impressed by this reminder of what had happened to their powerful neighbor. They also knew what it meant to be threatened by a powerful fleet. The Perry Treaty was concluded without bloodshed, but Yedo had been terrified by the appearance of a fleet equipped with guns which could blast to dust and splinters the strongest Japanese shore defenses. They did not know that Perry was under the most uncompromising orders not to use force. His actions gave no hint of this, for while he did not use force in the sense that he fired no guns, he presented the most terrifying threat of force the Japanese had ever seen.

Only a few months before this meeting Harris had been bemoaning the fact that he did not have the aid of a man-of-war and was fearful that he could accomplish nothing without one, but now he told Lord Hotta that, "by negotiating with me who had purposely come to Yedo alone and without the presence of even a single man-of-war the honor of Japan would be saved; that each point would be carefully discussed, and that the country should be gradually opened." As he had done in Siam, Harris insisted that he did not ask exclusive rights for Americans but assured Lord Hotta that any treaty which was acceptable to the President of the United States would be accepted by the other Western powers.

As a concluding argument he pointed out the danger to Japan of having the trade in opium forced on her and said he would be willing to conclude a treaty which would prohibit its importation.

I closed by saying that my mission was a friendly one in every respect; that I had no threats to use; that the President merely informed them of the dangers that threatened the country, and pointed out a way by which not only could those dangers be

217

averted, but Japan made a prosperous, powerful and happy nation.

Lord Hotta was obviously impressed by this presentation of the problem of his country's foreign relationships and said it was the most important matter ever brought before the Japanese government.

It would not be correct to say that Lord Hotta was convinced by Harris' arguments for he had already come to approximately the same conclusions. Of the many Japanese nobles who played a part in ruling the country, he was one statesman of broad vision who was not swayed by personal greed or ambition. Though his cold impassive face seldom indicated his emotions, there can be no doubt that his feelings for Harris approached those of friendship, because from the very first meeting he looked on Harris as a sincere friend of Japan.

Everything connected with his visit to Yedo had progressed with satisfactory speed, but the days following this important conference were filled with annoyances over petty and very unimportant matters. As in Shimoda, Harris found that while he had come to Japan with the responsibility of carrying on weighty and responsible negotiations he had to spend a good part of his time fighting for the human right to live a comfortable life. The Japanese brought up the old proposal to fill his quarters with officials and policemen whose ostensible purpose was to guard him against insult and injury and protect him against fire, but whose real duties were to spy on him and prevent his gaining access to anyone except the officials. There were long and unpleasant debates on the subject, wasting time that Harris wanted to spend discussing the treaty. He insisted that he had come to Yedo alone, that he wanted the government to place proper persons in his house but that it must be done at his request and not as their right.

After days of argument he finally won his point. An official letter admitted his right to full and complete control over the premises he occupied. The day after the settlement of this troublesome point the Japanese announced that they would accede to the request he had made a week or two previously for some ground on which to ride the horse he had brought with him from Shimoda. When they showed him the proposed exercise field, it was found to be only five yards wide and thirty yards long, about half the size of a Manhattan City lot. On his refusal to accept this tiny plot they offered another piece of about the same length but 25 yards wide. This was as useless as the other plot so after much further argument they agreed to allow him to ride on the military parade ground. Since there were objections to this on the part of army officers, the commissioners requested that he ride only twice a week and then for only one hour.

Day after day passed with these petty and tedious details and long conferences with individual members of the Council at which no progress was made. Harris was asked innumerable questions about the elements of political economy, commercial regulations and diplomatic procedure. Some of these questions were undoubtedly inspired by an honest search for truth. Others were on subjects with which the questioners were thoroughly familiar and were merely put in the hope that he could be tripped into a falsehood or an inconsistency or would commit himself in ways that could later be used to his disadvantage. Whatever Harris may have suspected as the reason for all of this questioning and cross-questioning, he met subterfuge with sincerity and answered all inquiries carefully and patiently. When his verbal explanations did not appear sufficient, he wrote long letters to the commissioners.

This is attended with more labor than can be well imagined, for I not only give them ideas for which, as they are new, they have no adequate terms, but the interpreter does not understand the Dutch terms when he hears them. Thus I am sometimes employed for hours in trying to convey a very simple idea. It requires an incalculable amount of patience to prevent my throwing the matter up in despair. But I know that every word I utter, every new idea I succeed in conveying, is at once carried to the Council of State, so I persevere in the hope that my labors will at last produce fruit, if not for me, at least for my successor.

The end of the year came with no reply from the officials to the proposal to start friendly negotiations for a new treaty nor any indications that they would make any move to follow the good advice he had given them. But he was not entirely disappointed with the progress made, for on January 1 he recorded the morbid fancy that he could not hope to see another New Year and then in the next sentence wrote: "I am thankful that I have been able to accomplish so much as I already have done for the honor of my country during the past year, and I hope that I shall be able to effectually open this country before the present one closes."

## CHAPTER XXI

## "CANNON BALLS FOR ARGUMENT"

DURING the first days of the year 1858 there was no indication from the Japanese commissioners in Yedo
that they were doing anything more than holding endless
conferences and talking about the proposed treaty in general, without in any way committing themselves. That, in
fact, is all they were doing at the frequent meetings with
Harris but the important and decisive conferences were not
those in which he took part but those held secretly in the
quarters of the hundreds of *daimyos.* A few days after his arrival in Yedo, Harris came to the conclusion that the Shogun
(whom he called the Tycoon and thought to be the Emperor) was only a lay figure; later he came to the further
conclusion that the august and distinguished commissioners
who were dealing with him, including even Lord Hotta
himself, were equally powerless. All that they could do and
all that they were doing was to note what he said, transmit
his remarks to the Council of State and avoid responsibility
by delaying discussion of the treaty as long as possible. He
did not know that his well-thought-out arguments for the
treaty were wasted on all but a very few unselfish patriots.
Each of the several hundred *daimyos,* military officials and
scholars who were eventually to decide the policy the country would follow had his own personal or family interests
to serve and in most cases it was these interests alone that
were considered.

In the midst of all these confused and conflicting interests which he sensed and only half understood, Harris might appeal to reason and justice and even to expediency but it was only through fear that the Japanese could be driven to a united decision just as it was through fear of the power represented by the Shogun that the warring clans of the country were kept at peace. He also had learned that in Japan as in Siam no confidences were ever respected; that he was surrounded by spies; and that every word he said to a Japanese official would be repeated to his colleagues; that one of the surest and most convincing ways of conveying an important message was to impart it in confidence.

This was the method he used when his old Shimoda friend, the Prince of Shinano, called on him almost a month after the original conference with Lord Hotta and the commissioners. Patience and courtesy having failed to bring any action, Harris determined to precipitate a crisis and did so by bitter complaints that he had now waited twenty-nine days for a reply to his very important communication to the Minister of Foreign Affairs but that no official notice had been taken of it, that the officials had not even named a time when he might expect a reply. Such treatment, he said, could not be submitted to. The President had sent him to Yedo on a most friendly mission, having in mind solely the benefit of Japan. The United States was not especially interested in the trade of the country and only wanted facilities for the repair and provisioning of ships; those had been granted by the Shimoda convention. "They must open their eyes and then they would see that I neither asked nor would I accept any favors from Japan."

He concluded with the statement that their treatment of him had shown that no negotiations could be carried on

222

unless the plenipotentiary was backed up with a fleet and could offer them cannon balls for arguments. As a final remark he said that unless something was done he would return to Shimoda. Although he did not say it in so many words, the inference was clear that he would there await the arrival of warships before continuing the negotiations.

The poor Prince of Shinano was terrified at the bold and threatening message he had to take back to the other more powerful *daimyos*. As he was on more intimate terms with Harris than any other official he had been specially appointed to look after the visitor and keep him in a harmless good humor; thus he might and probably would be blamed for this well-considered outburst of temper. He offered his assurances that no slight or insult was intended either to Harris or the President and took it upon himself to secure an immediate answer.

The message the Prince of Shinano brought to Lord Hotta and the other members of the Council had the desired effect. He was able to hurry back with a long and very reassuring reply. The commissioners admitted that Harris had just cause for complaint and then told a long story—not necessarily exaggerated—about the difficulties they faced. They said that they were enlightened and knew that what Harris had recommended was really for the best interests of Japan but their conviction alone was not sufficient. There were many others who had to be convinced including some who lived in distant parts of the country and had not yet replied to the letters which had been written to them. They urged Harris to continue to be patient. In Japan long deliberations were necessary before any important decision could be reached.

In spite of these assurances there were further delays

223

and it was not until Saturday, January 16, that the negotiations were resumed. The Japanese had learned to take advantage of the fact that Harris would transact no business on Sunday and often opened important negotiations on Saturdays as this would give them one entirely free day in which to devise answers to any new questions he might raise.

However, this conference began with the very satisfactory announcement that the demands for the residence of a minister at Yedo and also for the right of free trade had both been granted, the details of each arrangement to be worked out later. As to the matter of additional harbors, the decision was that as three had been opened and Japan was a small country the number would not be increased, but as Shimoda had not been found suitable it would be closed and another specified in its place.

Harris registered his objections to this limitation of harbors but did not waste much time arguing the matter. Instead, he proceeded to the more immediate task of setting up the legal machinery for carrying on the formal negotiations which had been completely neglected by the Japanese in spite of the careful explanations he had given them. As a matter of fact, it was a procedure with which they were not unfamiliar, for two of the commissioners had negotiated the treaty with Perry and none was without diplomatic experience. The procedure involved the appointment of commissioners and the exchange of documents setting forth the full powers of each party, all of which was satisfactorily arranged though not without many new and unnecessary explanations as to the proper diplomatic procedure. Actually the exchange of full powers was a meaningless formality. It soon developed that the commissioners had no power to do anything but listen to what Harris had to say, report each day's proceedings to the Council of State and attempt to get the Council to come to some decision and formulate a reply which they could take back to Harris. It was a one-sided arrangement, for while Harris had to come to his own decisions and was bound by his own statements, the commissioners accepted no personal or official responsibility. There was one detail of the arrangement which was eminently satisfactory to him. Instead of having to deal with all the "commissioners of the Voyage," two of them were delegated to carry on the negotiations and one was his old friend, the Prince of Shinano.

In the meantime, Harris had made all possible preparations for the conference by preparing a draft of the treaty he hoped to negotiate. He had, in fact, written this proposed treaty before leaving Shimoda, even before the question of his visit to Yedo was settled. He had talked to Sir John Bowring about it when in Hongkong.

I was anxious to take the initiative in presenting a draft, as, had the Japanese presented one, it would have been difficult if not impossible to reject it entirely, and to try to amend one of their performances would have made a piece of literary or diplomatic patchwork that would have excited the laughter of all who might have the misfortune to be compelled to read it.

At the first formal meeting with the commissioners Harris put on his full dress uniform "in honor of the signatures of the President and the Tycoon" which were to be exhibited at the exchange of credentials. At this exchange he was gratified to see that the Japanese were relaxing their intolerant attitude toward foreigners for the documents bearing the seal of the Shogun were handed to Harris for examination. When the Japanese commissioners met Commodore Perry they would not allow the document to go out of their hands, declaring that the Imperial Seal was so sacred that it could not be touched except by Japanese who had been specially designated to care for it.

After the formalities were over, Harris handed the commissioners a Dutch translation of the proposed treaty. In order to hasten the work of putting the text into Japanese, he suggested that the translators work in his quarters where they might have easy access to Mr. Heusken who would explain any words or phrases with which they were unfamiliar. The suggestion was adopted.

While all this was being done Harris was called upon to settle a new problem of American rights and privileges not specifically covered in either the Perry Treaty or the Shimoda convention. The American whaling ships were wintering in Hakodate and E. E. Rice, the uneducated U. S. Commercial agent who was stationed there, wrote to Harris that the men wanted rum and women and must have them. They were provided for the Dutch sailors at Nagasaki but denied the Americans at Hakodate. This was the first demand requiring what might be referred to as a broad interpretation of the "most favored nation" clause, written into the Perry Treaty at the suggestion of his missionary interpreter, Dr. Williams. Mr. Rice hinted that if the officials did not quit interfering with the sailors the latter might take action themselves and seize the port by force. As a matter of routine Harris presented the complaints to the officials and they readily agreed to the sailors' demands—as a health measure.

While the proposed treaty was being translated into Japanese there was another diversion at the castle which for the moment turned the minds of the *daimyos* from the problem of treaty making. Harris had told the Prince of Shinano that if a spot of white were to be found on any part of a dog, the tip of the dog's tail would be white. When he passed this information on to the castle, all the *daimyos* set their retainers to work trying to find a dog which would disprove this assertion. Every stray dog in Yedo was rounded up and examined and every one with a white spot was found to have a tail-tip of white. Harris gained a reputation for universal knowledge.

After the work of translating the treaty had been completed, the Japanese text was retranslated into Dutch and checked by Mr. Heusken, who returned it to its original English form so that Harris could compare it word for word. It was a long and tedious process and it was not until a week had elapsed that the work was completed and the discussion of the treaty itself was begun.

## CHAPTER XXII

# THE TRIALS OF TREATY MAKING

THE discussion of the actual text of the treaty was begun on January 25 and the devious and obstructive methods of the commissioners on the first day of the conference gave some hint of the trials which were to follow. Apparently the week Harris had spent in supervising the translation had been an equally busy period for the commissioners and the Council of State. The latter had anticipated every issue they could think of in connection with the treaty and had prepared what amounted to a voluminous book of instructions to which the two commissioners constantly referred, reading the most appropriate replies they could find. Two Japanese secretaries were employed taking down every word that was said.

In beginning what eventually developed into a very lengthy account of these proceedings Harris wrote that he would confine himself

to the main leading facts of the actual transactions, omitting the interminable discourses of the Japanese where the same proposition may be repeated a dozen times; nor shall I note their positive refusal of points they subsequently grant, and meant to grant all the while; nor many absurd proposals made by them, without the hope, and scarcely the wish, of having them accepted,—for all such proceedings are according to the rule of Japanese diplomacy, and he who shows the greatest absurdity in such matters is most esteemed. They do not know the value of a straightforward and truthful policy, at least they do not practise it. They never hesitate at uttering a falsehood even where the truth would serve the same purpose.

The first provision discussed struck the keynote to Japanese diplomatic policy which was to agree with apparent wholeheartedness to the provisions of an article and then insist on hedging it about with conditions which would make it inoperative. Thus the commissioners agreed to the acceptance of a minister to Yedo but insisted that he actually reside at Kanagawa or Kawasaki, two villages on the shore of the bay, and only come to Yedo when he had business to transact. The right of Consuls to travel in Japan had been conceded in the Shimoda convention but when this was reaffirmed in the draft of the treaty the Japanese ignored the fact that the right had already been granted and would have confined the Consuls' travel to business journeys. The minister was to be restricted in the same way.

As to trade with Americans, the commissioners said it had been determined to give them the same privileges that had been accorded to the Dutch and the Russians, here again ignoring the fact that under the "most favored nation" clause of the treaty made by Perry these privileges automatically accrued to Americans as soon as they were granted to others. But the provisions of the Dutch and Russian treaties were entirely unacceptable to Harris as they provided that all dealings must be through Japanese officials. Americans, they said, could not be allowed to travel in Japan, but must be confined to very strict limits of the open ports. Acceptance of these conditions would have placed American trade in Japan under about the same humiliating prohibitions as those suffered so long by the Dutch.

Harris made an indignant reply to these childish proposals. He said the suggestion to shut the minister out from residing in Yedo was highly offensive, that it would be much better to refuse to receive him than to offer a reception under such conditions. As to trade, he demanded that the promise of the Shogun, "that freedom of trade should be granted," be made good. He said that he was convinced that the people of Japan were anxious to trade with foreign countries and that if any objection did exist it was confined to the *daimyos* and the military, two classes of people who in all countries usually opposed any improvement in the great body of the people. The treaties negotiated by the Dutch and Russians would never be accepted by the President because of the humiliating conditions which they imposed. For example they gave the Japanese authorities the right to impose fines of the most outrageous character, and for light offenses both ship and cargo could be confiscated.

The two commissioners could find no answers to these arguments in their books of reference and consulted together for a long time. Finally the Prince of Shinano asked permission to unfold the details of what he said was a very private and confidential matter.

He then said that of the sons and brothers of military men, none enjoyed any rank except the eldest son; that they all received a military education, being taught the art of war, the use of weapons, etc. They had no pay, nor any prospect of advancement in life. They were supported in idleness by the head of the family, as their positions forbade their devoting themselves to any useful avocations, and they had no hope of honorable employment. Their only distinction consisted in their right to wear two swords.

From these habits of idleness many of them fell into bad courses, became dissipated, drunken brawlers and bullies; and that when their conduct became too outrageous they were disowned and cast off by their families. In this condition they form a class called *ronin* which corresponds to bravo, bully, rowdy and loafer. The Government has just discovered a plot among these *ronin* against the American Ambassador (what they intended to do to me I could not learn), and the Government had that morning arrested three ringleaders of the conspirators and had them now in prison.

The Prince of Shinano having made this story as terrifying as possible triumphantly concluded that Harris must now see that the residence of the American minister in Yedo would be certain to cause disturbances and therefore it would be much better for him to live at Kawasaki or Kanagawa.

It struck Harris as a peculiar and most suspicious circumstance that he should have lived in peace and quiet in Yedo for more than two months and that this plot should have been unearthed just on the eve of these discussions, so he declined to be either frightened or impressed. In fact he refused to argue the matter and in the little time remaining for the day's conference he suggested that they take up the draft of the treaty and give a general reply to each article. The reply of the commissioners was a monotonous negative to every proposal except the one article which provided for the religious freedom of Americans residing in Japan. This was the one issue on which Harris as well as Secretary Marcy had anticipated the most determined opposition.

231

When the conference was resumed the following day the commissioners insisted that they had been misunderstood. They had not refused the minister the right to reside in Yedo but had merely suggested that Kawasaki or Kanagawa would offer more suitable places for his residence. They therefore agreed to this article, but then insisted that the treaty not go into effect for a period of more than three years. When Harris rejected this they asked him to give his secret promise that no minister be sent before that time. The commissioners had told Harris that special guards had been placed around his residence to protect him from those murderous *ronin*; indeed, he heard them making the rounds every night until the question of the residence of the minister was settled, when they disappeared.

Week by week the tedious negotiations proceeded. In spite of his resolve to confine his journal to an account of actual accomplishments Harris filled many pages with details of the wriggling evasiveness of the commissioners. However, the daily sessions were soon discontinued as these placed too great a physical burden on the officials who had to discuss each day's proceedings with the Grand Council, receive their instructions, and then be ready for the next session. The pretense that they had full powers was soon abandoned and it was more and more clearly apparent that the Grand Council itself did not dare go in opposition to the wishes of the *daimyos* who had conflicting and often antagonistic interests. The only consistent person was Harris who pursued his course in the full confidence that what he was doing was for the best interest of Japan, as well as of the United States. Except in a vague and indefinite way he had no conception of the complicated conflicts which were going on behind the scenes. He did not know that the

Shogunate was fighting for its existence. It was probably fortunate for Harris that he was ignorant of the complexities of Japanese politics as he was enabled to pursue his course with a singleness of purpose otherwise difficult to achieve.

In their search for pretexts and points on which to haggle and bargain, the Japanese commissioners overlooked one item which would have been very embarrassing to Harris if they had brought it up. In a burst of friendly enthusiasm, Perry had assured the Japanese that the inland waterways of the United States would be open to them and that they would be free to work the gold fields of California.

Point by point, some of the various provisions of the treaty were agreed to, usually as the result of long and sometimes stormy argument; but often, to Harris' great surprise and for no apparent reason, the commissioners would suddenly concede a point which they had been stubbornly disputing for days. With the exception of the one provision respecting religious freedom, all the articles of the treaty were troublesome but the most difficult negotiations were over the additional ports which were to be opened for trade. Shimoda, which had been of little value when opened as the result of the Perry Treaty, was rendered completely valueless as a result of the tidal wave. The Japanese agreed to substitute some other port in its place, but refused to go any farther than that. Harris had prepared to make some concessions in this matter by demanding more ports than he expected to get. His list included eight seaports and he also insisted on the opening of Kyoto and Yedo to trade.

This question of additional ports compelled the Council of State to give very serious consideration to the conflicts of interest and authority between the Shogun and powerful *daimyos*. As each of these ports lay within the domain of some one *daimyo*, the proposal to open it to foreign trade was more or less dependent on his consent. So jealously did some of these powerful *daimyos* guard their hereditary rights that even the Shogun himself could not visit certain parts of the country without the permission of the local feudal ruler. While a few wanted foreign trade because of the greater revenues it would assure them, others were just as resolutely opposed.

There was unexpected opposition to the proposed opening of Kyoto and the commissioners tried to discourage Harris by saying that it was a poor place, with a small population and no manufactures of any importance. They assured him that silk was woven in not more than twenty houses and that no lacquer ware was made there. Kyoto was the residence of the Mikado—the powerless emperor —and when Harris spoke of the veneration in which he understood this mysterious figure was held the commissioners roared with laughter and spoke contemptuously of him. "They say he has neither money, political power, nor anything else that is valued in Japan. He is a mere cipher."

In view of the great theoretical power that the Emperor of Japan holds today this contemptuous reference to him, made just eighty years ago, is very interesting. The commissioners were not exaggerating when they said that he had no power, for Japan had been governed for more than two centuries by the Tokugawa Shogunate. But at the time Harris was in Yedo the Shogunate was no longer the powerful institution of the past; it was supported only by those who were bound to it by self-interest, while a powerful and growing party was planning its overthrow under the pretense of restoring the Emperor. Harris of course had no inkling of this conflict for he believed that the Shogun who had received him in such imperial state in Yedo was actually the Emperor. The commissioners assured Harris that the opening of Kyoto to foreign trade would result in a revolution but they did not explain why.

As the negotiations proceeded, Harris gained concessions at almost every conference. From his limited knowledge of the internal politics of the country he was justified in assuming that these victories were due to his own persistence and the presentation of arguments which the Council of State could not confute. On the other hand, a more important factor was probably found in the growing conviction on the part of the *daimyos* that if they did not make a treaty with Harris they would soon be faced by the allied French and British fleets which had captured the Chinese forts at Canton and were now threatening an attack on Peking. While to Harris it appeared to be a personal triumph for persistence and reason, it was also a triumph of fear.

At the end of the second week in February the commissioners begged to be excused for a few days as the approach of the New Year holiday period made it necessary for them to draw up their annual reports. But the treaty was so far advanced and so many points had been agreed to that it was decided to go ahead with making clean copies of the text, and translations into Japanese of the alterations and amendments.

In view of the friendly relationship which now exists between America and Great Britain and the relations of the two countries toward Japan, it is strange to read of the satisfaction with which Harris records the fact that the Japanese agreed to provide ports at which American naval vessels could store provisions and thus be free from reliance on Hongkong. He said: "I consider this clause of immense importance, as now the depot can be removed from that wretched place Hongkong, and the stores out of the power of England."

## CHAPTER XXIII

## AN APPEAL TO THE MIKADO

THE two commissioners were five hours late when the conference was resumed after the end of the New Year holidays. On their arrival at Harris' residence they did not take up the matter of the treaty but began a long statement in which they recounted a detailed history of the negotiations, starting with the audience with the Shogun. Even before their long statement was translated into Dutch and then into English, Harris knew that something was amiss, not only by their anxious expressions but their constant reference to the *daimyos*. They repeated all of the old objections to the opening of the country and the opposition to any change in the ancient customs. The apparently pointless narrative went on for more than an hour, then they arrived at the meat of the story.

The draft of the treaty as it stood when the conference was suspended for the holiday

had been submitted to the *daimyos* and instantly the whole Castle was in an uproar. Some of the most violent declared that they would sacrifice their lives before they would permit such great changes to be made. The Council of State had labored incessantly to enlighten these men; had pointed out to them not only the policy, but necessity there was to make the Treaty if they would avert the ruin of the Kingdom, etc. They had brought over some, but others still remained obstinate; that the Government could not at once sign such a Treaty, except at the expense of bloodshed; that they were sure the President did not wish to bring any such evil on Japan, etc., etc.

The commissioners probably did not tell Harris all the details of the opposition aroused. To the *daimyos*, who were absolute masters of their own domains and thought only in terms of military might, it was unthinkable that any surrender should be made to this strange barbarian from America. Even the suggestion was an insult to their pride. Many of them struck back blindly. One of the belligerent *daimyos* was irate at the suggestion that the combined naval forces of England and France could compel Japan to sign a treaty. He offered to defeat England and France and all the rest of the world if the Shogun would loan him the Castle of Osaka to serve as a headquarters and advance enough money to pay for the building of a small fleet. He was so much in earnest that he wrote Lord Hotta a long letter about it. But as soon as this angered warlord was given a high position in the Shogunate, his opposition ceased.

At the end of the long statement by the commissioners there came the greatest surprise of all when Harris learned that what they wanted to do was to delay the signing of the treaty until some member of the Council of State could go as ambassador to the Mikado in Kyoto, whom they now referred to as "The Spiritual Emperor," and secure his approval. Less than three weeks before this they had laughed contemptuously at the mention of the Mikado's name, saying that he was a mere cipher with no political power. Now they assured Harris that the moment his approval of the treaty was secured, the *daimyos* must withdraw all opposition!

Neither Harris nor any other foreigner at that time, nor

Interview between Lord Elgin and the Ministers of Japan
Chief interpreter Moriyama kneeling in center

A distant view of a portion of Harris' visit to the capital

for some years later, had any but the vaguest idea as to the complex constitution of the government of Japan. Even the Dutch, who had enjoyed a monopoly of the trade of the country for so many years and looked on the Shogun as the Emperor, did not know that he was technically an usurper and the only powers he held were those which had been delegated to his family by the imperial clan in 1615. For almost two centuries the power of the Tokugawa family had been unquestioned. The Shogun ruled supreme and the Emperor in his seclusion at Kyoto was half-forgotten. But the Tokugawa rule had been weakened by a succession of feeble and witless Shoguns and now many of the other powerful *daimyos* were plotting its overthrow.

It was Harris himself who was unwittingly giving these enemies of the Shogunate their opportunity for action, for they could find both unity and a popular appeal in opposition to the opening of Japan to the foreigner. But the Council of State, which represented the Tokugawa power, assumed that if the approval of the Emperor could be secured, then the ground would be cut away from the opposition by destroying its political expediency. On the conclusion of the Perry Treaty the Shogun had revived the ancient formula of securing the imperial assent and the Mikado had proven as indifferent to political affairs as his ancestors had been in the past. He had given his approval as a matter of routine.

But in the meantime the courtiers who surrounded him began to sense the new political opportunities presented to them by the weakening of the Shogunate. For the first time in the long reign of the Tokugawa family the Kyoto courtiers offered opposition. At the time the commissioners were explaining this situation to Harris two minor officials from Yedo had been in Kyoto for ten days trying to explain matters to the Mikado. They had left Yedo full of confidence that the errand they were undertaking was a mere formality as this was all that similar missions had ever amounted to. But they found a powerful exclusion party dominating the court of the Mikado and were entirely unsuccessful though they persisted in their attempts and remained in Kyoto for more than a month. All that the mission did accomplish was to widen and more clearly define the breach between Yedo and Kyoto.

As they did not wish to disclose to Harris the real position of the Shogun or to confess that he as well as Commodore Perry had been systematically and successfully deceived as to the identity of the Emperor of Japan, the commissioners' explanation of this extraordinary situation was attended with a great deal of difficulty. But they were quite sincere in their assurances that the approval of the Mikado was a mere formality which would present no difficulties. There was no precedent for the Mikado's doing anything but place the seal of approval on whatever the Shogunate proposed, just as the Emperor today automatically approves the measures proposed by his ministers. When Harris asked the commissioners what they would do if the Mikado refused his assent, they replied in a very decided manner that "the Government had determined not to receive any objections from the Mikado."

Heusken, who had listened to the gossip of the other interpreters, told Harris that vast sums of money had been sent to Kyoto to bribe the courtiers and the Emperor and that still greater sums would be sent if it were found necessary.

The commissioners said the treaty would be accepted

practically as it stood and proposed that they go ahead with the discussion of the various minor amendments, proceed with it until it was completed and engrossed and ready for signature. When this was done Harris might amuse himself in any way he liked, until the approval of the Mikado had been secured and the treaty signed. If he wanted to return to Shimoda the government would send him there and bring him back by steamer. Coming at a time when he was beginning to see an end to his long and difficult labors, this news climaxed a series of disappointments and discouragements which had begun the day he landed in Shimoda. But he seized on the one hopeful suggestion the commissioners had made, that they proceed with the treaty until its terms had been agreed on.

After he had spoken his mind very plainly about what he referred to as "childish tactics," consideration of the treaty was resumed but very little progress was made. The first article had been agreed to, then revised and agreed to again, and this process had been repeated so many times as to make it appear that the commissioners' objections had all been exhausted. But now they threshed over the old ones and so managed to spin out the first day of the resumed conference that when, late in the afternoon, the meeting was abandoned because of weariness, nothing had been accomplished except to leave in doubt questions which had been definitely settled.

The conferences which followed were little more successful. Harris had brought plenty of champagne with him and although he drank none himself, he served it to the commissioners. Sometimes it did not produce the desired effect and the commissioners became garrulous and obstinate.

The delegates from the Council of State were still in

Kyoto but momentarily a report from them was expected though with the passage of each day things grew less hopeful. In the meantime no opportunity to waste time was overlooked. The commissioners had agreed to fire a salute of twenty-one guns on February twenty-second in honor of Washington's birthday but as the day approached they informed Harris that the salute would be fired near Kawasaki, about eight miles from his residence, adding that this was the nearest point at which cannon could be fired. When Harris said he had heard howitzers fired in the neighborhood, they replied that these must have been from guns belonging to the *daimyos*. Harris declined to travel eight miles to hear the salute fired, and they blandly suggested that he send Mr. Heusken, who could return and tell him about it. Eventually the matter of the salute was dropped but the commissioners had accomplished their purpose of delaying a further consideration of the treaty to which they had already verbally agreed.

The Prince of Shinano in a private call on Harris assured him that the government, as represented by the Council of State, was acting in good faith and was anxious to conclude the treaty, that the mission to Kyoto was bound to succeed and that when the assent of the Mikado was secured, the opposition of the *daimyos* would instantly cease. He admitted that a very large majority of the *daimyos* were opposed to the treaty and the government was constantly working on them. Some of them had been convinced but others were obstinate and would yield only to the opinion of the Mikado. The Prince of Shinano had lied to him as had all the other Japanese officials but on this occasion Harris believed he was speaking the truth.

Harris at length suggested the following plan: that they go ahead with the minor amendments to the treaty, have it engrossed and ready for signature. Then the Council of State or the Minister of Foreign Affairs would write him a letter saying that the treaty was completed and ready for signature but for certain important reasons of state the actual signing of the treaty would have to be delayed for sixty days. When this had been done Harris would return to Shimoda, prepare his dispatches to the government and then, when notified of the approval of the Mikado, would return to Yedo and the treaty would be signed. In his journal he wrote:

I do not see what I can do better under the peculiar circumstances in which I am placed. If I get the written promise of the Government that *the* Treaty (not a treaty) shall be signed by a certain day, I do not see but it is as binding on them as the signature of the Commissioners to the Treaty itself.

The suggestion that this procedure be followed had been made in an informal conversation with the Prince of Shinano and it was immediately accepted by the Council of State. Lord Hotta did not wait for the conclusion of the treaty but wrote the letter at once. In this letter he stated that the negotiations were ended, the treaty was ready for signature, and after explaining the embassy to Kyoto concluded: "wherefore a time of two months will be required, on or before which time the Treaty shall be signed." Although in this letter Lord Hotta agreed to sign a treaty which had not yet been concluded, he was not committing himself unwittingly, for the limits to which the two commissioners could go had been very clearly defined by the Council of State. He was determined to get the matter settled without further delay. The other emissaries had not yet returned; he was setting out himself for Kyoto to lay the matter before the court of the Mikado.

243

## CHAPTER XXIV

## "THE TREATY WILL BE SIGNED"

With this letter from Lord Hotta agreeing to the signature of the treaty and with the assurances of the commissioners that with a few minor amendments the treaty was acceptable as it stood, Harris resumed the negotiations in better spirits. But his hopeful mood did not survive the first few meetings. As the details were developed these "minor amendments" proved to be so numerous, so troublesome and so absurd that the whole treaty had to be gone over again point by point.

The preamble only was accepted without question. The first article provided that "all diplomatic and consular officers shall have the right to travel freely in any part of the Empire of Japan" and there was more trouble about this than about any other article. It looked for a time as if the whole treaty would be wrecked over this one provision and Harris offered to strike it out entirely, leaving the officers to claim their rights "under the law of nations." But after wasting many hours, the Japanese finally accepted it.

The uproar of the *daimyos* over the surrender of their ancient rights, honors and privileges and the opposition which had developed at Kyoto frightened the commissioners anew. Each of them was saddled with the obligations of old personal friendships and feuds. Although they may have been perfectly sincere in their efforts to work for the best interests of Japan as a nation their minds were influenced by the claims of the *daimyos* to exclusive jurisdiction in their own domains, their jealous objections to infringement of their ancient rights, and the desire of some to embarrass the Shogun's government by any means in their power. Many who were at this time the most outspoken in their opposition to any concession to the foreign barbarians later admitted with surprising frankness that they knew the policy of seclusion must and should be broken down but that they opposed the treaty as a means of rallying support to the party which opposed a continuation of Tokugawa rule. The problem of the Council of State was not to negotiate a treaty which would be for the best interests of Japan, but a treaty which would on the one hand meet the demands of the foreign powers as represented by Harris and, on the other hand, arouse the least objection from the *daimyos*. There was also the new political factor, the awakened ambitions of the Emperor in Kyoto, which had to be taken into consideration.

In justice to the Japanese officials it must be said that Harris, like all foreigners, had but a vague idea of the tangled ramifications of the feudal government, did not fully appreciate their difficulties and often charged the officials with bad faith when they were following a course from which they could not deviate. The fact that they were such ready, though not always clever, liars prevented an understanding. They had told him so many falsehoods that now he did not believe them when they told him the truth. He had come to the conclusion, justified by his experience, that with the Japanese officials "to lie is the rule; to tell the truth is the exception."

Thus the commissioners were undoubtedly telling the truth when they said that the Shogun (meaning of course the Council of State) was in favor of the treaty, believing it to be in the best interests of the country, that the small *daimyos* did not dare to openly oppose the government but shielded themselves under the opinion of the greater *daimyos*. Some of the latter were in favor of the treaty but the great majority were violently opposed to it. The members of the Council of State had a larger vision than the average *daimyo*, while Lord Hotta was a statesman far in advance of his generation.

Washington's Birthday was a gloomy day for Harris. The strain of the long and unsatisfactory negotiations and the bad meals served him by his Japanese cook were beginning to tell on him. After successfully demanding the withdrawal of the guards from around his house and coming to a fairly satisfactory arrangement for the exercise of his horse, he lived in tedious self-imposed seclusion, taking his exercise by walks in the courtyard. In two months he went out of the house only once and that was to pay an official visit to the Minister of Foreign Affairs. One reason for this seclusion was that he felt it might help him maintain the "exalted rank" to which the Japanese had elevated him. Perhaps a stronger reason was the fear that if he went about the city he might unwittingly offend some of the powerful *daimyos* through ignorance of the etiquette to be observed. His seclusion, uncomfortable as it was, was probably a very wise precaution. Retainers of the feudal lords did not hesitate to plunge a sword into anyone who failed to prostrate himself on what they considered to be appropriate occasions. As he makes no note in his journal of the salute of twenty-one guns having been fired, it may be assumed that the Japanese had forgotten his request. The day was marked

246

only by the fact that the Prince of Shinano called on him with more proposed amendments to the treaty.

They are of various classes. Some are absurd, others mischievous, and not one that is of the least benefit to Japan by adding to her security or honor. The insertion of some would obscure what is now clear, and many would excite laughter. The tone of all the amendments is unfriendly, and haughty, and calculated to make the Treaty unacceptable.

They had not as yet decided on the tariff, consequently the subject of tonnage dues, import and export duties, and fines for violations of customs and shipping regulations were still left open promising a really plausible excuse for further interminable delays.

When the formal conference was opened on February 23 Harris was thoroughly disheartened; he felt that he would completely fail in making a treaty which would be acceptable to his government but would not give up. He opened the discussion by saying that he had carefully considered all the proposed amendments and told the commissioners that

some were a mere change of words, others rendered the meaning obscure, many will open the door for disputes and difficulties; that the change of a word in one Article sometimes required the alteration of many Articles, as all must agree; that many of the amendments showed a very unfriendly spirit, and that the insertion of what they proposed would cause the Treaty to be rejected.

They then took up the various articles of the treaty and much to Harris' amazement and delight, all opposition and obstruction disappeared. The old objections and arguments which he had heard so often were not even men-

247

tioned. The commissioners appeared to be as anxious as he for a speedy and satisfactory conclusion of the work. The troublesome question of the ports to be opened and the boundaries of the ports was settled without quibbling. Harris had contended for the opening of eight ports but was content to accept six at which Americans could live and carry on trade. He failed in his attempts to secure the rights of residence in Kyoto. The amendments were disposed of in rapid order and by 5 P.M. the treaty was agreed to as well as most of the regulations. It was the most satisfactory day he had had; the Japanese for the first time in his experience seemed to be in earnest and had made decisions promptly and reasonably.

The only important matter not settled on this busy and successful day was that of duties. The commissioners proposed a uniform export and import duty of 12½ per cent, probably because this was the levy in China. Harris argued vainly against an export duty and finally compromised on an imposition of 5 per cent on all Japanese productions exported as cargo, thus freeing ship supplies from the imposition. He then proposed and the commissioners accepted a graduated scale of import duties with intoxicating drinks of all kinds significantly heading the list of 35 per cent. American business men who were principally interested in shipping and the whaling industry were given a distinct advantage. "While American trade was taxed at 5 per cent it left British manufactures at 20 per cent and French wines at 35 per cent to provide the bulk of the revenue for the Japanese government."*

While there may have been other reasons for this change of front on the part of the Council of State, whose opinions

* Tyler Dennett in *Americans in Eastern Asia.*

were reflected by the commissioners, there is good reason to believe that it was inspired by Lord Hotta in preparation for his visit to the Emperor at Kyoto. The two unsuccessful emissaries who were still there had gone to ask approval of a treaty which had not yet been negotiated, a document which they could only describe in general terms. As hitherto the approval of the Emperor had been nothing more than a formality which was granted as soon as it was asked, it had not been thought necessary to go into details. In fact the two emissaries had not been of high rank and the official note which they carried with them was very brief, gave no more specific details of the treaty than had been contained in the short speech of the Shogun on the occasion of Harris' reception.

The Emperor's party was in a belligerent mood and affected to be insulted by the low rank and vague proposals of the envoys. The mere fact that the envoys had been sent at all was evidence of the growing weakness of the Shogunate, for it was clearly within the legal right of the Shogun's government to sign the treaty without reference to the Emperor. Faced by this unexpected opposition from the Emperor's party, Lord Hotta determined to go to Kyoto prepared to answer any questions that might arise and to present the Emperor with a *fait accompli*.

On February 27 all details of the treaty had been cleared up and a clean copy was given to the commissioners. The work had been completed just in time for on that day Harris fell so violently ill that he asked to be sent to Shimoda by boat. He had been ill from the time of his arrival in Yedo, but kept going through the strength of his willpower and succumbed only when the strain of the long ordeal was over. He rallied enough to sign both copies of the treaty and write a long letter to the Secretary of State, then collapsed. His mind was a blank during the period that Lord Hotta was attempting to secure the Mikado's approval of the treaty.

For weeks Harris hovered between life and death. In a personal letter written after his recovery he said:

The Emperor and the Council of State manifested the utmost solicitude during my illness. His Majesty daily sent me very kind messages, with presents of fruit and little delicacies to tempt my appetite. He also sent two of his best physicians to attend me. The doctors sent a daily report of my situation to the court, and on receipt of a bulletin stating that I could not recover, the Emperor issued peremptory orders to the physician to cure me, adding that the safety of their heads depended on my recovery.

The journal which was broken off by this illness was never resumed except for a few fragmentary notes made during May and June. A careful reading of the portion of his journal covering the period from the time he landed at Shimoda shows quite clearly that he was in constant fear that he would not survive one of his frequent attacks of illness and he carefully recorded each day's events so that in the event of his death his successor could take up the work where he left off. The final entry reads:

"The Treaty is to be signed."

His work had been accomplished and it was no longer necessary for him to provide a journal for the guidance of his successor.

## CHAPTER XXV

## SIGNED ON A BATTLESHIP

LORD HOTTA left for Kyoto to secure the approval of the Emperor to the treaty with every confidence of success. But he remained there month after month thwarted on every side by the hitherto powerless and subservient Kyoto court. He made an eloquent plea to the throne in which he paraphrased much that Harris had said about the foreign relations of Japan the day he gave the Japanese so much good advice. Lord Hotta pointed out the changed conditions in world affairs and the dangers which threatened Japan if she persisted in the policy which had brought such grief and humiliation to China. With a breadth of vision lacking in his colleagues and with unbounded confidence in the destiny of his country he portrayed to the Emperor the opportunities for world domination which were presented by the opening of Japan. This idea that Japan was to rule the world was not a new conception. Less than three hundred years before this Hideyoshi, the great popular hero of Japan, had embarked on a grand imperialistic campaign to conquer all Asia, place the Emperor of Japan on the throne at Peking, and divide India between the Japanese feudal lords. His campaign failed because of unexpected Chinese resistance but his dream was familiar to every Japanese. Hoping to stir the Emperor with ambitions beyond the petty intrigues of his courtiers, Lord Hotta told him:*

* *Lord Hotta, Pioneer Diplomat of Japan,* by Henry Satoh, Tokyo, 1908.

The present condition of the world shows that it is lacking in a ruler sufficiently powerful and virtuous, under whom all countries could be united. Among the rulers of the world at present, there is none so noble and illustrious as to command universal vassalage, or who can make his virtuous influence felt throughout the length and breadth of the whole world. To have such a ruler over the whole world is doubtless in conformity with the Will of Heaven. Before the countries of the world can be unified under a great ruler, international conditions show the necessity of establishing relations among the nations, either by forming an alliance with those equal in virtue and power, or by concluding treaties of amity and good will. . . .

The utmost effort should be made to become thoroughly acquainted with the affairs of other countries with which treaty relations have been established, and in establishing relations with foreign countries, the object should always be kept in view of laying a foundation for securing the hegemony over all nations. . . .

Our national prestige and position thus assured, the nations of the world will come to look up to our Emperor as the Great Ruler of all the nations, and they will come to follow our policy and submit themselves to our judgment. This ideal realized, the Ruler of Japan will have accomplished a deed commensurate with the great responsibilities he owes to Heaven and Earth.

Lord Hotta's idea of a world which would be unified and kept at peace by the overpowering might of one ruler was the only one which he and other Japanese statesmen could conceive. It had only been by the domination of a series of dynasties of powerful Shoguns that the warring clans had been kept at peace. The idea that Japan should play this role in world affairs has never been forgotten for a moment, has been the inspiration of the country's ardent patriotism. Every sign of progress by Japan, every indication of weakness or disunity on the part of other countries has been accepted as evidence of this great destiny.

This portrayal of future power and glory failed at the time to stir the lethargy of the Emperor or to weaken the opposition of the reactionary court officials who surrounded and controlled him. In reply to Lord Hotta's insistence about the treaty he gave nothing but evasive and inconsistent answers. The Emperor said that the Yedo officials were empowered to take care of such matters—and then said the approval of the *daimyos* should be secured. He would not himself give the approval which was needed to bring the reactionary *daimyos* into line.

The courtiers with a courage which was new and strange to them were openly and violently hostile. They armed themselves and threatened the life of the Prime Minister and would not leave his residence until he had agreed to their demands. Their courage was not equal to an attack on Lord Hotta for they feared the vengeance of the Shogun, but they did make distant threats. As a result of the intimidation of the Prime Minister the reply of the Emperor was finally changed so as to leave no discretion to the Yedo officials in the matter of the treaty. The imperial reply denounced the Shimoda convention as a national outrage and instructed the Shogun to secure the approval of the three houses of the Tokugawa family and also of the *daimyos* before again asking for the imperial sanction. Lord Hotta was ordered to return to Yedo with this reply but evaded the order by sending a substitute.

With great tact he brought the subject up again only to find himself facing the stone wall built of the ignorance, stubbornness and prejudice of the Kyoto court. The Emperor told him that the national defenses should be put on an efficient footing "lest the refusal to grant any more than the concessions made in the Shimoda Treaty be made a cause for war." His final suggestion was that if the *daimyos* could not arrive at a decision in any other way they should leave the question to the oracle of the great Shrine of Ise.

Later Japanese historians have had a difficult time explaining the absurdity and the contradictory terms of the many orders issued by the Emperor at this period and have generally repudiated them as false on the ground that they were too ridiculous to have emanated from the mind of a ruler of such recognized virtue and wisdom.

The continued illness of Harris relieved the commissioners of the unpleasant duty of telling him about the failure of Lord Hotta's mission and he had no information that the plans had not worked out according to schedule. With the approach of the day set for the signing of the treaty he insisted on returning to Yedo and, in spite of the objections of his Japanese physicians, was carried on board the boat. He arrived there on April 17 and to his great disappointment found that Lord Hotta had not yet returned from Kyoto. The situation was much the same as it had been when he left Yedo for Shimoda at the beginning of March. It was in fact much more serious for the long stay of Lord Hotta in Kyoto showed that the Emperor's party was stronger than anyone in Yedo had realized. His Japanese friends hardly recognized Harris for he was like a skeleton and his hair was perfectly white. The worried Council of State asked for a further delay of twelve days. He bitterly reproached the Shogunate with the deception which had been practised on him and said he would

Dinner given to the Japanese Commissioners by Admiral Perry on board the Powhatan

be held accountable to the President for the false position in which he had allowed himself to be placed. He said that if the Yedo government had no power to sign a treaty, he would go to Kyoto himself and negotiate directly with the Mikado. His illness made such a journey impossible, so he stayed in Yedo.

It was not until June sixth that Lord Hotta returned from Kyoto, invited Harris to his residence and frankly told him all about the situation. The unexpected opposition at Kyoto had brought unity to the party supporting the Shogunate for the visit of Harris to Yedo had precipitated the struggle between the Shogunate and the Emperor. Many of those who had secretly plotted to undermine the power of the Tokugawas changed their tactics when confronted by the possibility of a restoration of the Emperor with a new combination of powerful families in control. Lord Hotta gave Harris his assurances that the Council of State had fully decided to sign the treaty, that they would crush the opposition by force if necessary, but if Harris would consent to a further delay the matter could be settled without bloodshed—which would be unavoidable if the treaty were signed at once.

Lord Hotta proposed, through the commissioners, that the signing of the treaty be postponed for three months. Harris suggested that they sign at once and date it three months hence, but this they refused to do. Finally, September 4, 1858, was agreed upon, the second anniversary of the date he had hoisted his consular flag at Shimoda. Harris agreed to this further delay only with the understanding that no treaty with any other nation would be signed until thirty days after the signing of the American treaty.

His insistence on this condition was motivated by a

stronger reason than his perfectly natural desire that the treaty which had cost him so much pain and labor should be the first one. During his Yedo negotiations he had not continued his correspondence with Curtius, the Dutch commissioner at Nagasaki, but when all the details had been arranged and he had the written promise that the treaty would be signed on April 21, he wrote to Curtius to that effect. The latter arrived in Yedo on April 23. When he learned that the American Treaty still awaited a signature he offered to negotiate a treaty on behalf of his government which would be "acceptable to the *daimyos.*" The Council of State was eager to accept this proposal, for it would mean a compromise which would extricate them for the moment from their political difficulties. But Harris felt sure that any treaty negotiated under such conditions would be a patchwork affair which would not serve either the interests of Japan or the foreign powers.

Having secured the written pledge of the Council that the treaty would be signed on September 4, Harris returned to Shimoda on June 18. In a letter to Secretary Cass forwarding a copy of the Dutch translation of the pledge, he said: "This document may fairly be considered as a virtual execution and ratification of the Treaty."

Harris was prepared to spend an anxious and lonely summer in Shimoda, hoping that the treaty would be signed on the date set but fearing that something would happen.

Sick and weak and dispirited by the disappointing turn of affairs, his return to Shimoda was unhappy and he found the place even more lonely than before. News of the death of his old friend, Captain Drinker, added to his despondency. There was no hint of this in the carefully prepared official dispatches, but in a despairing letter to Mrs. Drinker, he wrote: "You cannot conceive the mental isolation of a solitary being like me; nor can you imagine the void that is created in my soul by the want of some object to protect and love, and to be loved by in return."* His house was full of dogs and pet birds, on which he lavished the most tender care.

But he had been in Shimoda only a little more than a month when his tedious wait was dramatically interrupted. On July 23 the *Mississippi*, one of the American squadron which had accompanied the British and French fleets on their expedition to North China, arrived at Shimoda with startling and important news. The British had suppressed the Sepoy mutiny in India; the allied British and French fleets had defeated the Chinese troops in North China and the Chinese government had been compelled to sign a treaty granting all the demands of the foreign powers.

Though this was news to Harris it was rather late in arriving as the Chinese troops had been defeated and the British treaty signed by Lord Elgin and the Chinese commissioners nearly a month previously. The important fact was that with their troubles in China settled, the British and French fleets were on their way to Japan to negotiate a treaty. The Russian squadron which had, like the Americans, been peacefully observing events in North China, was also on its way. The *Mississippi* was soon followed by the *Powhattan*.† On this latter man-of-war Harris pro-

* Janvier collection of letters in Manuscript Division, New York Public Library.

† Commodore Tattnall who arrived in Shimoda on the *Powhattan* had not remained entirely neutral in the attack of the British and French fleets on the Chinese forts at the mouth of the Peiho. He violated American neutrality by towing a boatload of British marines into action and became famous by his explanation that "blood is thicker than water."

257

ceeded to Kanagawa where he dispatched a letter to the Yedo officials telling them of the news from China and urging "the very great importance of having the Treaty signed without the loss of a single day."

From the time he began his negotiations Harris had repeatedly pointed out to the Japanese that if they persisted in their attempts to bar out the foreigner, the walls would be battered down by the fleets of the foreign powers as was being done in China; that it was very much better for them to sign a treaty such as he proposed than to wait and have a treaty forced on them. They were probably better informed than he was about events in China but by no means so confident that the allied fleets would succeed. His news that the foreign fleets had departed China and were on their way to Japan probably confirmed news they already had.

The Yedo officials were undoubtedly thoroughly alarmed, for the two commissioners arrived on the *Powhattan* at midnight. In spite of the fact that it was contrary to all precedent to fire a salute at that hour, Commodore Tattnall received them with a salute of seventeen guns whose distant thunders were doubtless heard at Yedo by many officials who thought that the assault on Japan had begun.

At the midnight conference on board the *Powhattan* the commissioners still hesitated when Harris urged them to sign the treaty at once. They said that as all of the *daimyos* had been notified that the treaty would be signed on September 4, it would cause "confusion" to sign it any earlier. Harris assumed an indifference he probably did not feel and replied, in effect, that it did not matter to him, that he had simply given them his candid advice, that if they did not care to follow it he would return to Shimoda and wait until September 4, and they could deal with the other powers themselves—but he pointed out that they were pledged not to make a treaty with another country until thirty days after his treaty had been signed. The commissioners were more worried and distressed than they had ever been before. They could not find their usual escape in evasion or delay. They were no longer timorous about the American Treaty but fearful that they might have to make even greater concessions. They asked Harris to write a letter guaranteeing that the British and French would accept his treaty, which he declined to do. But he did ease their minds by a letter stating his *belief* that the British and French would sign the treaty and offering his friendly services in the event that there were any difficulties.

The conference lasted until the early hours of the morning, when the commissioners returned to their boat to translate the letter Harris had written. They had no time to go to Yedo for consultation and instructions, for they were back again a little after noon on July 29—and the treaty was signed. In spite of the plans Harris had made for a treaty which would be drawn without a hint of coercion, it was signed on an American gunboat after all.

Commodore Tattnall hoisted the American and Japanese flags and fired a salute of twenty-one guns.

## CHAPTER XXVI

## JAPAN OPEN TO THE WORLD

THE *Powhattan* had hardly sailed for home with the signed copy of the treaty before the fleets of the other powers—British, French and Russian—arrived from North China. Having brought the haughty Manchu court to its knees, the British and French were now prepared to settle the other important outstanding problem of the Far East —trade with Japan—and in no mood to stand any nonsense from this Asiatic power. Harris had in the meantime returned to Shimoda where the envoys found him living in hermit-like seclusion. Lord Elgin, who was in command of the British expedition, called there on the way to Yedo and Harris gave him invaluable advice and suggestions, doing everything in his power to repay the British for the help he had been given by Sir John Bowring. In spite of Harris' assurances that the other powers would be satisfied with the treaty he had made, the Japanese officials were frightened. They attempted to negotiate with Lord Elgin at Nagasaki and again at Shimoda—sought in every way to prevent his going to the Bay of Yedo where the Russian fleet was already anchored.

The British ships left Shimoda at daylight the morning of August 12 and at midday passed the Russian squadron anchored off Kanagawa. The British fleet did not stop here but steamed on up the bay. The officers derived a good deal of satisfaction from the fact that they got to

Yedo before the Russians. As he had no interpreter who would be of any value in Japan, Lord Elgin had borrowed the invaluable Mr. Heusken. He also borrowed the palanquin which had been specially constructed for Harris' journey to Yedo. The fact that the British plenipotentiary arrived in Yedo not only with the interpreter but also the palanquin of the American Consul-General was very confusing to the Japanese officials but was of great help to the British. The palanquin gave Lord Elgin great reflected prestige and Heusken enabled him to make short work of the Japanese formalities. They could not try any of their old tricks on Heusken and they were too occupied to invent many new ones.

As Harris had said in a letter to Bowring, Lord Elgin's work was done for him. Whatever difficulties he might have encountered were obviated by the presence of Mr. Heusken, who was thoroughly familiar with the treaty and on this occasion acted more as a first secretary than an interpreter. It was probably the only time in history that an American citizen held an important post in a British diplomatic mission. The official historians of the mission expressed great appreciation of his services but never learned to spell his name correctly and always referred to him as Mr. Herksin. The British were very grateful to Harris also for his friendly help. In appreciation Queen Victoria sent him a gold snuffbox.

The negotiations between the British and the Japanese were friendly to the point of being frivolous. In China Lord Elgin had bullied the frightened Manchu commissioners, shouted at them, pounded the table and talked menacingly of firing a few more broadsides from the British men-of-war. In Yedo the politeness was excessive. There were luncheon- and tea-parties and pleasant excursions into the country, and undoubtedly new Japanese records were established in the consumption of champagne. After the long and tedious work he had done in China, Lord Elgin's visit to Yedo was little more than a pleasant holiday. It is no wonder that he recorded his impressions of his brief visit to Japan as "a green spot in the desert of my mission to the East."

As the provisions of the Harris Treaty, except for unimportant details, were acceptable to each side, there was nothing to negotiate, but the Japanese delayed matters as much as possible in order to keep their promise to Harris not to sign another treaty until thirty days after the signature of the American treaty. By August 20 there was nothing more to decide, for all of the provisions of the treaty had been agreed to. There was no reason why the treaty should not be signed the next day or the day after, but they managed to postpone the signing for six more days, until August 26. That was a few days short of the thirty days promised, but no doubt the date was fixed with the full agreement of Harris who had been following the negotiations with a paternal interest. When the long and tedious formality of affixing all the signatures and seals to the different copies of the treaty had been concluded, all sat down to a banquet sent them by "the Emperor." It was not until several months later that they learned that the Shogun, whom they and all other foreigners thought was the Emperor, had died on August 16, a few days after their arrival in Yedo. His death was concealed until September 12. Fortunately Lord Elgin and the other emissaries had not embarrassed the Japanese officials by demanding an audience as Harris had done.

Other treaties were made with Russia, France, Holland and Prussia—all of them following the Harris model with a few minor and unimportant changes. Any hopes Harris might have entertained that he had served the cause of temperance by providing a high import duty on alcoholic beverages were dashed by the French who saw to it that the duty was reduced to a nominal figure. In the negotiation of all of these treaties Harris played a helpful and friendly part. His position was unique. He was not only the *doyen* of the diplomatic corps; he was the only member of the corps. Mr. Heusken continued to be handy man for all the diplomats and served as interpreter for the Prussian mission.

Harris remained in his little temple at Shimoda waiting for the treaties to be ratified and for the date of the opening of the legation at Yedo. For that occasion the *Mississippi* returned to Shimoda on March 1, 1859, and Harris, who had in the meantime been appointed Minister to Japan, was the honored guest of the ship on a four months' cruise in Japanese waters. He visited Nagasaki for the first time and returned to Yedo, where on July 7 he hoisted the flag over the American Legation which had been established in the Buddhist temple—known as the Shrine of Virtue and Happiness.

The difficult and important work of negotiating the treaty with Japan had been accomplished but there was no relaxation for the newly appointed American Minister. In his isolation at Shimoda he had complained about not receiving any letters, but now he was deluged with them. The Department of State which had neglected him so grievously now found many things for him to do. American merchants and manufacturers with visions of a big new market deluged him with inquiries and with requests to do petty errands. The manufacturers of Hostetters Bitters sent him some samples with the request that he present them to the Emperor in the hope that they could get a testimonial. The samples were forwarded through the State Department and it was necessary for him to write an official dispatch explaining the impropriety of the attempt to exploit the famous bitters in this way. He had to investigate charges that American naval officers were engaging in trade in Japan and this was varied by a charge that he was speculating in Japanese gold. The Japanese were interested in modern armaments and called on him to secure samples of all the different types of arms in use in America. He had but little clerical help and worked far into the night laboriously answering letters and writing dispatches to the Department of State.

These routine duties were soon disturbed by the political upheaval which followed the signing of the treaties. The cry "expel the barbarian" was a popular one and was used to the best advantage by the growing party, which was not so much concerned with the expulsion of the foreigner as with the overthrow of the Shogunate and the restoration of the Emperor to his ancient theoretical power.

This movement culminated in January, 1861, in the murder of the inoffensive and obliging Mr. Heusken. There was no reason, either personal or political, why he should have been the victim of the plot which was simply to kill some foreigner so as to further embarrass the Shogun's government and bring about reprisals from which the government would be the principal sufferers. Perhaps he was killed because of a convenient opportunity or perhaps because his was, except for Harris', the most familiar foreign figure in Yedo. In any event, the French and British ministers fell unwittingly into the plot by hastily closing their legations, retiring to the safety of Yokohama and insisting that the few other foreigners living in Yedo follow their example. There was loud talk of reprisals against what was wrongly interpreted as an anti-foreign uprising. Harris alone appeared to realize the political significance of the murder and declined to give his sanction to any reprisals against the government. His colleagues were bitter in their recriminations. In a personal letter* dated July 1, 1861, Harris wrote:

You have no doubt heard of the murder of my secretary, Mr. Heusken, last January. This event caused a great panic among my colleagues who thought their lives were in danger and they fled to Yokohama for safety. I remained here alone and my action probably prevented some very aggressive measures from being adopted by the French and English.

My course has been approved by the foreign community both in Japan and China, and the Japanese are loud in their thanks to me, saying that I had prevented the horrors of war from being brought on them. This affair has broken off all intercourse between me and the French and English legations, which makes my position here a very isolated one. I go down to Kawagawa once in a while and visit the missionary ladies . . . who are very agreeable persons, but with this exception my life is almost as isolated as it was while living in Shimoda.

The loneliness of his position and the seeming ingratitude of the other diplomats to whom he had extended many favors must have galled him acutely, for he made constant references to it in his letters. Writing again on September 16, he said:

* Letter to Miss Kate Drinker, Manuscript Division, New York Public Library.

My colleagues, the English and French ministers, have taken up their residence at Yokohama . . . and they only come to this city when they have special business to transact. This leaves me once more alone in this vast city and of course makes my life here very solitary. Yet on the whole I am not sorry for the absence of my colleagues. They are both exceedingly nervous men—are very unpopular with the Japanese—and were constantly getting into some new difficulties which always gave me more or less trouble.

The British and French ministers were insistent that he demand a large punitive indemnity for the murder of Heusken, but Harris took the view that payment of an indemnity would not reach the guilty parties and contented himself with a demand for $10,000 which was paid to Heusken's mother.

Harris' courageous action in remaining in Yedo and his refusal to join in punitive action against the government not only provided a fitting climax to his career as a diplomat but also raised him to the highest pinnacle of Japanese esteem. Doubtful and suspicious at first, they were slowly but firmly convinced of his fairness and his disinterested friendship, and partly because of his luck they came to have a veneration for his political astuteness. From his first interviews with the officials he had continued to warn them that unless they opened the country to foreigners of their own free will, they would be compelled to do so at the point of a gun. And the arrival of the British, French and Russian squadrons came just at a time to impress these warnings on them. In retrospect then as in retrospect now they could see that his advice had been both sound and unselfish, that Japan was very much the gainer by having followed it. His refusal to accompany his colleagues in a flight to Yokohama gave him, in the eyes of the Japanese, a perhaps exaggerated reputation for bravery. Though he remained in Yedo, he was carefully guarded.

The name of Townsend Harris is as familiar to Japanese of today as the name of Lafayette is to Americans. Legends and plays have been built up about him and every spot he visited in Japan has become one of historic importance. He provides the central figure in a number of popular Japanese plays. Japanese dramatists have paid him the doubtful compliment of inventing the character of a geisha who, according to the play, loved him devotedly and consoled him in his loneliness at Shimoda.

## CHAPTER XXVII

## THE LONELY EXILE RETURNS

IN HIS letter to President Pierce in which he made a formal plea for appointment, Harris assured him that he had a "perfect knowledge" of the social banishment and mental isolation he would have to endure in Japan and that he was prepared to meet it. He pointed out that he was a single man "without any ties to cause me to look anxiously to my old home, or to become impatient in my new one." When he made this statement he was giving assurances about a condition of life he had never experienced, for he had always been surrounded by friends and the words "loneliness" and "isolation" were only words in the dictionary. He had left old friends in New York but found new ones in the Far East. Even the void in his life caused by the death of his mother had been partly filled by the friendship of Mrs. Drinker, the motherly wife of his dearest friend in Hongkong.

Nor could he imagine the completeness of the isolation which would engulf him in Japan. His inhospitable reception at Shimoda, followed by months of unfriendly suspicion, obstruction and veiled but obvious hostility was something he could not have anticipated. Here it appeared that friendship did not spring from the human emotions but grew hot or cold, following the orders of one's superiors. It was turned on and off like water in a tap. He had many reasons to believe that in Japan both friendship and truth were commodities which were not dispensed freely but traded in with cunning and skill. He had to live in Japan for some time before he learned that lovable human attributes were to be found in the common people though not in the superior classes who ruled them. But this discovery did not relieve his loneliness, for in his official position he was restricted to associations with officials and had constantly to be on guard in everything he said or did.

In his many letters to his personal friends he said little about these troubles but there are illuminating though sparing references to them in his journal and in his letters to the sympathetic Mrs. Drinker. Each holiday brought memories of happy days he had spent in New York and memories of old friends, and made him more keenly conscious of his loneliness.

Nor did Harris anticipate that the State Department would contribute to his isolation and discomfort by forgetting to provide for the regular call of ships bringing him mail and supplies, or neglect to work out a method whereby he could collect his salary and contingent expenses and meet the bills which fell due to the Japanese. At the time he was invited to go to Yedo he was out of both food and money and deeply in debt to the Japanese officials through whom he was compelled to make his purchases. In a letter he wrote while waiting in Shimoda for Lord Hotta to conclude his negotiations at Kyoto he said:*

I am very unpleasantly situated as it regards my pecuniary condition. I cannot negotiate my bills in Japan at any price and am therefore compelled to send them to China. I have already sent bills for $5,500 but have not been able to get the

* Letter of July 16, 1858, to Mrs. Sandwich Drinker in Manuscript Division, New York Public Library.

first dollar of returns owing to the want of conveyance for the money. I have now in my pocketbook bills for $4000 which are of no more value here than so much waste paper. I loaned to the Russians $1000 in December, 1856, which they promptly repaid at Hongkong the following month. That money also remains there for want of means of sending it to me. The remainder of the money which I brought with me to Japan was exhausted nearly a year ago and since that time I have been reduced to the mortifying necessity of asking credit from the Japanese for my necessary daily supplies.

I am in debt to my servants, and was disturbed in what were supposed to be my dying moments by their murmur for their pay. Can you imagine anything more unpleasant? I am out of flour, butter, lard, hams, bacon and in fact all articles of foreign production and am reduced to the Japanese diet of rice and fish. For this reason I have not purchased a single article for my friends, as I am unwilling to increase my pecuniary obligations to the Japanese except for what is absolutely indispensable.

He secured some supplies from the *Powhattan* but in spite of the improvement in his diet his health continued very poor. After the signing of the treaty he was anxious to return home even though he knew that his appointment as Minister to Japan was a foregone conclusion. "I have nothing to return with," he wrote Mrs. Drinker. "If the government shall allow me a just compensation for the treaties I have made with Siam and Japan I will invest it in an annuity and return at once."

At the time this letter was written the Siam Treaty had been ratified more than a year and American merchants had established themselves in Bangkok. When the treaty was under consideration Senator Seward introduced a bill providing for compensation of $10,000 for Harris. Secretary

Marcy wrote a letter in support of the bill stating that Harris had received no salary until his arrival in Shimoda. The Senate ratified the treaty and passed the bill for compensation but no action was taken on it by the House.* At the end of 1860 the matter was still unsettled but Harris, worn by illness, could stand the loneliness and isolation no longer. With the ill feeling which existed between him and the other diplomats in Yedo, the death of Heusken, and the political turmoil which was turning Japan into armed camps of rival feudal partisans, he was even more lonely than he had been in the little fishing village of Shimoda. "I am very homesick," he wrote, "and want to return and it is my present intention, if my life is spared, to return early in 1861. For the past eleven years I have only spent 82 days in the United States."

He had set this date for his return in the hope that he would be able to save enough money to live on for what he thought would be the few remaining years of his life. There was one way in which he could add a few hundred dollars to this sum and that was by being recalled from his post, in which case his salary would continue until he arrived in the United States; whereas if he resigned, the salary would stop the moment he was relieved from duty. But the administration refused to recall him, and in the autumn of 1861 he was still in Yedo, further saddened by the news he had received about the Civil War and the deaths of some of his old friends. "My friends are rapidly falling under the inevitable doom and I must soon follow," was his characteristically fatalistic comment.

In the meantime the controversy over the slavery ques-

* It would appear, from a careful search of the records of Congress, that Harris was never paid for his work in Siam.

tion had put Lincoln into the Presidency and he appointed Seward as his troublesome but brilliant Secretary of State. Harris' appeal to him for an order of recall was also refused and at length (July 10, 1861) he sent his resignation to President Lincoln. It was more than a formal resignation, for it was accompanied by such convincing representations regarding his failing health and advancing years that there was nothing to do but accept it. The Japanese government which seven years before had made such persistent efforts to compel him to leave the country now asked the American government to induce him to remain, and showered honors on him.

He returned to New York in 1862, where he lived modestly but comfortably on the annuity he had purchased. When Grant was put in command of the Union armies, he sent the general the sword which the Shogun had presented to him on his departure from Japan. He joined the Union Club where he found the food to his liking; helped to found the New York Society for the Prevention of Cruelty to Animals. He was always at home to visitors from Japan. In spite of his constant complaints of ill health, he lived until 1878 when he died at the age of 74.

 He lived, in fact, just long enough to die a forgotten man, for the turmoil of the Civil War and the Reconstruction which followed drove from the mind of the public all memory of the great work he had accomplished in Japan.

# BIBLIOGRAPHY

COSENZA, DR. MARIO EMILIO, *The Complete Journal of Townsend Harris*, Doubleday, Doran, New York, 1930.

GRIFFIS, W. E., *Townsend Harris, First American Envoy to Japan*, Houghton Mifflin Co., Boston and New York, 1895.

DENNETT, TYLER, *Americans in Eastern Asia*, Macmillan, New York, 1922.

FOSTER, JOHN W., *American Diplomacy in the Orient*, Houghton Mifflin Co., Boston and New York, 1904.

NAKAMORA, KAJO, *Prince Ito, the Man and Statesman*, Arrako, New York, 1910.

GOWEN, HERBERT H., *An Outline History of Japan*, Appleton, New York, 1932.

BANCROFT, HUBERT HOWE, *The New Pacific*, Bancroft, New York, 1915.

TAYLOR, BAYARD, *Library of Travel*, Scribners, New York, 1893.

HAWKS, DR. FRANCIS L., *Narrative of the Expedition of an American Squadron to the China Seas and Japan*, Washington, 1856.

LONGFORD, JOSEPH H., *The Story of Old Japan*, Longmans, Green, New York, 1910.

OLIPHANT, LAURENCE, *Lord Elgin's Mission to China and Japan*, Harpers, New York, 1860.

BAKER, GEORGE E., *Life of Seward*, Redfield, New York, 1860.

GRIFFIS, W. E., *The Mikado's Empire*, Harpers, New York, 1877.

WOOD, DR. WILLIAM MAXWELL, *Fankwei*, Harpers, New York, 1859.

SATOH, HENRY, *Lord Hotta, the Pioneer Diplomat of Japan*, Habubukan, Tokyo, 1908.

BOWRING, SIR JOHN, *The Kingdom and People of Siam*, London, 1857.

ALCOCK, RUTHERFORD, *The Capital of the Tycoon,* London, 1863.

HILDRETH, RICHARD, *Japan—as it Was and Is,* Boston, 1855.

WILLIAMS, S. WELLS, *The Middle Kingdom,* Scribners, New York, 1883.

TREAT, PAYSON JACKSON, *Early Diplomatic Relations of the United States and Japan, 1853-1865,* Baltimore, 1917.

KING, MOSES, *King's Handbook of New York,* New York, 1892.

VALENTINE, DAVID T., *Valentine's Manual of Old New York,* New York.

MEYERS, GUSTAVOS, *History of Tammany Hall,* New York, 1917.

COSENZA, DR. MARIO EMILIO, *The Establishment of the College of the City of New York as the Free Academy in 1847, Townsend Harris, Founder,* New York, 1925.

WILSON, R. R., *New York Old and New.*

LOSSING, *History of New York City.*

New York City Directories for the years 1812 to 1853.

*Annals and Occurrences of New York City and State in the Olden Time,* New York, 1846.

Encyclopædia Britannica.

Dictionary of American Biography.

Appleton's Annual Cyclopædia.

Numerous Government publications, Senate Documents, etc.

## MANUSCRIPTS AND DOCUMENTS

Journal of Townsend Harris in the Library of Congress, Washington.

Janvier Collection of Letters of Townsend Harris, Manuscript Division, New York Public Library.

Files of the Bureau of Appointments, Department of State, Washington.

Papers connected with the settlement of the estates of John and Townsend Harris.

## PAMPHLETS, NEWSPAPERS AND MAGAZINE ARTICLES

MORRIS, ROLAND S., *Townsend Harris. A Chapter in American Diplomacy,* distributed by the Japan Society of New York.

*An American Shrine in Tokyo,* Proceedings of a Memorial Meeting for Townsend Harris by the Phi Beta Kappa in Japan, Tokyo, 1931. Distributed by the Japan Society of New York.

New York World. March 1, 1878.

New York Times Magazine. December 28, 1919.

Harper's Weekly for the years 1857 to 1859.

Quarterly of the New York Historical Society.